Fortress · 13

OSPREY
~HING

Norman Stone Castles (1)

The British Isles 1066–1216

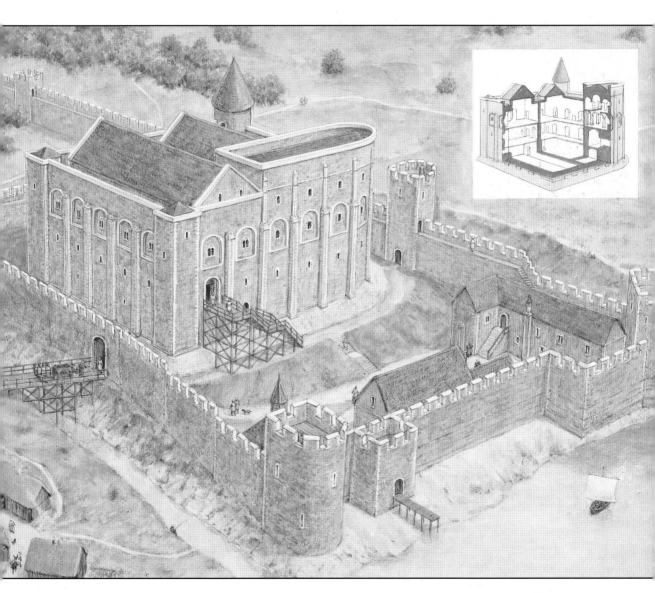

Christopher Gravett · Illustrated by Adam Hook

Series editors Marcus Cowper and Nikolai Bogdanovic

First published in Great Britain in 2003 by Osprey Publishing, Elms Court, Chapel Way, Botley, Oxford OX2 9LP, United Kingdom.
Email: info@ospreypublishing.com

ISBN 1 84176 602 X

Editorial by Ilios Publishing, Oxford, UK (www.iliospublishing.com)
Maps by The Map Studio, Romsey, UK
Index by Alison Worthington
Design: Ken Vail Graphic Design, Cambridge, UK
Originated by Grasmere Digital Imaging, Leeds, UK
Printed and bound by L-Rex Printing Company Ltd.

03 04 05 06 07   10 9 8 7 6 5 4 3 2 1

A CIP catalogue record for this book is available from the British Library.

FOR A CATALOGUE OF ALL BOOKS PUBLISHED BY OSPREY MILITARY AND AVIATION PLEASE CONTACT:

Osprey Direct UK, PO Box 140, Wellingborough,
Northants, NN8 2FA, UK
Email: info@ospreydirect.co.uk

Osprey Direct USA, c/o MBI Publishing, PO Box 1,
729 Prospect Ave, Osceola, WI 54020, USA.
Email: info@ospreydirectusa.com

www.ospreypublishing.com

Dedication

To Jane and Joanna, for suffering numerous visits to stately piles.

Artist's note

Readers may care to note that the original paintings from which the colour plates in this book were prepared are available for private sale. All reproduction copyright whatsoever is retained by the Publishers. All enquiries should be addressed to:

Scorpio Gallery, PO Box 475, Hailsham, East Sussex, BN27 2SL, UK

The Publishers regret that they can enter into no correspondence upon this matter.

Conversion table

1 inch	2.54cm
1 foot	0.3048m
1 yard	0.9144m
1 mile	1.609km

All pictures are by the author, unless otherwise indicated.

Contents

Introduction

It has been argued that the English castle began with the Anglo-Saxons (who by 1066 should perhaps be more properly termed the Anglo-Danes), pointing out that they sometimes occupied defensive structures. However, an opposing viewpoint holds that the English castle began with the Normans. Since a castle is a home as well as a stronghold, the communal burhs seen in England before the Norman Conquest, and designed to protect a number of people, do not qualify. Only a thegn's private dwelling, with ditch and palisades, suggests possible continuities with the castles of the Normans. Contemporaries of the Normans, such as Orderic Vitalis, certainly thought of castles as a novelty and the lack of them in pre-conquest England as a contributing factor to defeat; yet it may be only their use as centres of seigneurial administration by the Normans that truly sets them apart from the defended houses of the English thegns. The use of a tower to display the lord to his subjects, evident in some early Norman stone gateways, certainly seems to echo the Anglo-Saxon burhgeat with an opening in its upper storey.

Timber castles spread far and wide after the conquest, and were quick to erect in a hostile land. They had been in use, at least in north-western France, from about the 9th or 10th century. As the Carolingian Empire tottered and Charlemagne's sons and grandsons squabbled over his territories, Viking raiders

The White Tower in the Tower of London, begun c.1077, as it appears today. The large windows replaced the originals in about 1700. The apse of the Chapel of St John has resulted in the rounded south-east corner.

took full advantage to probe down the river systems and strike quickly. Central government was in disarray and local lords were thrown back on their own resources. The feudal system was emerging, with knights doing homage to a powerful man and promising to fight for him in exchange for land, or a place in his household. Castles emerged to protect the lord and the warriors who lived within them. Even in this period, however, the stone tower could occasionally be seen. Expensive and time-consuming to build, some may have started out as solid houses of stone, whose security could be increased by the addition of a tower if necessary. The most famous survivors are Doué-la-Fontaine and Langeais, both in the Loire Valley. The former seems to have begun life in about 950 as a ground-floor hall, before being altered to a tower with a first-floor entrance after a fire: Langeais, built perhaps in 994 or 1017, may also have been intended as a castle hall rather than a tower.

Stone towers are often called 'donjons', a term rooted in the latin word *dominus* referring to a lord. Originally it seems the word might have meant the lord's own area of a castle, not necessarily the great tower itself, but by the end of the Middle Ages it certainly referred to the great tower. The word 'keep' is not seen in England until the 16th century, when it appears in 1586 in Sidney's *Arcadia*. All castles were a statement of a lord's power,

The tower at Chepstow, Gwent, built *c*.1072, has a thin wall on the strongly defended river side, but still has a first-floor entrance, an import from first-floor halls in Normandy.

and large stone towers built in England would have seemed like skyscrapers to an Anglo-Saxon population mainly used to wooden buildings. The Norman dukes certainly had a large tower in their capital at Rouen, which formed part of the palace (now vanished). It is perhaps not surprising, therefore, that when the Normans arrived in England, they soon began to include a few stone towers amongst the large numbers of castles being constructed to hold down the conquered country. One of the first was a fortified palace (begun *c*.1077) in the south-eastern corner of the City of London, being so impressive that it gave its name to the whole castle – the Tower of London. Others followed, at first few in number, for the time it took to construct a large stone structure (the White Tower did not reach its full height until after 1100) meant that the earth and timber castle was a far more urgent requirement. We have noted how Orderic viewed castles as a contributing factor to Norman success, and castles were certainly of great value. Troops from within could hold down an area, sortie to snipe at or harry the supply lines of an enemy force, or join up with similar garrisons to form effective opposition. Conversely the enemy would need to take hostile castles as they progressed, to prevent such action. However, recent research has suggested that for the most part there was little danger of serious revolt after 1069.

As William consolidated his new kingdom, castles were soon being erected in towns and cities – sometimes planted as the army passed through to crush revolt elsewhere – to control the populace and to command any road or river traffic flowing through the place. They were built along the south coast, to guard ports and river estuaries and to deter any future invasion. However, many seem to have appeared simply to replace the headquarters of English lords. As castles proliferated down the social ladder (there may have been about 600 by the turn of the 12th century), the Norman kings may have lost some control over the building activities of their vassals. Some castles spawned a new town around their base, one of the most successful being Ludlow in Shropshire, built by Roger de Lacy. At first this was a deliberate policy of the king, but magnates soon took up the idea, and by 1100 some 21 new towns had been created. Lords also desired to

The interior of the tower at Chepstow. The beam holes for the first floor are clearly visible; the far end may have been screened off to form a private chamber. The pointed arch at the end plus the walls above the round openings are early-13th-century insertions, as are the pointed window openings.

build castles as heads of their honours (their collective estates), and so we find fortresses springing up in smaller places such as Richmond, Yorkshire, where the Earl had his main seat.

Royal control of castles may have been more a matter of public sponsorship, and evidence of 'licensing' during Stephen's civil wars seems to imply that some lords were merely asking for royal confirmation in uncertain times, while actual 'adulterine' castles are rarer than once thought. When Henry II took power in 1154 the unlicensed castles he wanted to destroy were those of political enemies, rather than exemplifying a general royal control policy. However, Angevin kings were interested in acquiring castles, not least because castles – especially those held by a sheriff – gave stability and political clout.

Castles also proliferated in areas of unrest, part-icularly the borders with Wales and, to a lesser extent, Scotland. Marcher lords guarded roads and rivers with castles, and soon the areas along the borders were thick with fortresses, often on Roman sites. A number of these were stone fortresses from the start, such as Chepstow in Gwent. As the Normans penetrated South and North Wales, they created castles there too. However, the number of castles successfully besieged raises the question of whether their military role was considered their most prominent function. In Scotland most of the new castles built by the incoming Normans in the 12th century were of earth and timber: as in England, they were ideal when speed of construction was necessary. The kings of Scotland seem to have actively supported the settlement of Anglo-Normans in Galloway, to help control the area. Stone castles were rare until the early-13th century, when they became more common in the Lowlands. Cobbie Row's Castle in Orkney, which claims to be the oldest stone castle in Scotland, was not built by the Normans but by a Norse chief in about 1145. Probably the rectangular donjon at Castle Sween on Loch Sween is the earliest in Norman style, but only dates to about 1220. Similarly in Ireland, when Henry II launched his invasion in 1169 the castles that appeared were usually of motte and bailey type. So useful were they that timber towered castles were still being built in the late-12th and early-13th centuries, alongside still rare stone fortresses such as that at Carrickfergus. However, despite Gerald of Wales writing that the new castles in Ireland were to subdue the natives, groups

RIGHT **The Tower of London as it may have looked c.1100**

The Normans utilised the old Roman city wall, repaired by the Anglo-Saxons and seen here running down to and then along the banks of the River Thames, to form two sides of their new castle. Ditches and palisades around the other two sides formed an enclosure: in 1097 William Rufus replaced the palisades with stone walls. Previous to this, in around 1077, Gundulph, Bishop of Rochester, began work on a new tower that would not reach its full height until about 1102. The eastern curved corner betrays the internal apse of the royal chapel of St John, a feature not initially planned, as the foundations reveal an original squared corner. The apsidal corner echoes that of the contemporary castle at Colchester. The first-floor entrance to the castle was reached by timber stairs. Internally (see inset) the 'White Tower' (a name deriving from the 13th-century whitewashing it received) had its two floors divided into two rooms of unequal size, usually defined as 'hall' and smaller 'chamber'. A third room, the smallest, led from the chamber: on the second floor this room was the chapel. There is no evidence for a kitchen. In addition to its role as a contemporary skyscraper aimed at impressing the populace of London, the palace of the Tower may have been intended primarily for important functions, with the luckier guests brought up through a series of increasingly impressive rooms to meet the king.

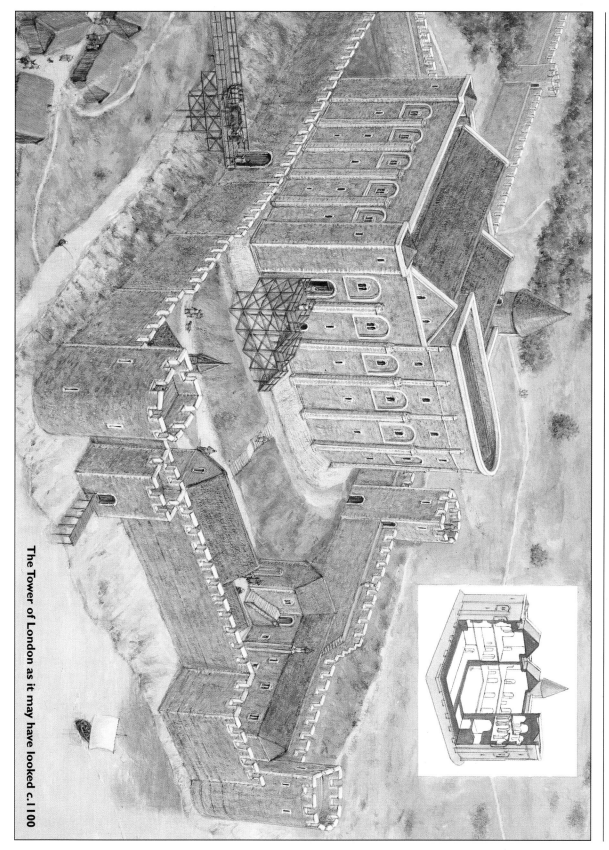

The Tower of London as it may have looked c.1100

7

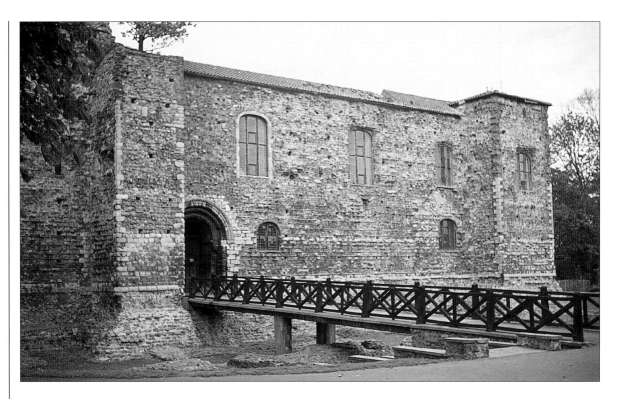

Colchester Castle, Essex, has the largest plan area of any Norman castle in England. It is similar to the White Tower, though quite low. It is not known if it ever had additional upper floors.

of mottes were usually placed in frontier areas, probably to check raiding. The erection of most other castles, especially those built of stone, suggests a desire to demonstrate a Norman lord's presence. Only later were additional fortifications needed to resist external threats.

Gradually, more stone fortifications were used to strengthen defences, perhaps at first comprising a simple ring wall, but also occasionally a donjon. As well as these, other elements – gatehouses and mural towers of stone – that had been built from the outset gradually increased in number. Donjons multiplied during the 12th century until many castles could boast a great tower of lesser or greater proportions. In the later-12th century the donjon would be the subject of experimentation, as polygonal and cylindrical versions appeared.

In recent years there has been much study of Norman castles and in particular of the donjon. A rather different picture is beginning to emerge of some of these great monuments but it may never be known exactly how they were employed. The uses these buildings were put to have for many decades been rather stereotyped. The various floors have frequently been labelled – often without a shred of evidence – as basement, entrance and/or garrison floor, great hall and private solar. Recent review of the known facts has caused a major rethink of key aspects such as whether some towers were built for different reasons, and how they were actually employed. In a number of cases we have to say simply that we do not know for certain and probably never will. We can, however, make educated guesses.

Although the later donjons were built under the Angevin kings, the Norman male line having ended with Stephen in 1154, their architecture is 'Norman' Romanesque and their builders often of Norman stock; thus this book will cover the period up until King John's death in 1216.

Chronology

1066	Norman Conquest of England and accession of William I.
1068	Siege of Exeter.
1087	Death of William I. Accession of William II.
1088	Sieges of Tonbridge, Pevensey and Rochester.
1100	Death of William II. Accession of Henry I.
1135	Death of Henry I. Accession of Stephen.
1136	Siege of Exeter.
1139	Siege of Devizes.
	Siege of Ludlow.
1140	Siege of Lincoln. Battle of Lincoln develops and Stephen captured.
1142	Siege of Oxford. Matilda escapes Stephen's siege lines.
1154	Death of Stephen. Accession of Henry II.
1158–65	Henry II invades Wales.
1169–71	Henry II invades Ireland.
1173–74	Scots invade northern England and besiege Carlisle, Brough and Prudhoe.
1189	Death of Henry II. Accession of Richard I.
1190	Richard leads the Third Crusade to the Holy Land.
1199	Death of Richard I. Accession of John.
1204	Loss of Normandy.
1215	Magna Carta is sealed.
	Civil war sees rebels and Prince Louis of France besiege Rochester.
1216	Prince Louis besieges Dover.
	Death of John. Accession of Henry III.

Castle Acre, Norfolk; the remains of the chalk and flint house built by William de Warenne within the earthworks date from the late-11th century, probably before 1085. The door and windows were blocked, floors removed, walls thickened, a curtain wall erected and the timber gatehouse replaced by a stone one. The addition to the north half of the building in 1140–60 turned the 'country house' into a donjon.

Design and development

Stone castle design

Many Norman stone castles were adaptions of existing earth and timber castles, by the simple exigency of pulling down the timber palisade around the bailey and replacing it with a stone wall. Some ring-works were changed to an enclosure protected by a wall in this way. In a number of towns with existing Roman defences, some repaired by the Anglo-Saxons in their turn, the invading Normans made use of the sturdy Roman stone walls, with their famously hard cement. By siting a castle in the corner of such urban defences the Normans acquired two ready-made walls, and they only needed to provide the other two to create a square, rectangular or oval bailey. The great stronghold of the Tower of London started life in this way, as did Exeter Castle. At the Tower of London the first Norman defences were of earth and timber on the other two sides, until a stone curtain wall replaced the palisades in the reign of William Rufus. There is no obvious sign of a motte, though it is possible that the area originally contained an Anglo-Saxon ditch, now entirely destroyed. At Portchester in Hampshire the Normans cut off a corner of the Roman fort in similar fashion.

Many ring-work castles have either lost their early stone defences or they now form only a part of the defences that survive. They were usually quite plain, comprising a wall thick enough to provide a fighting platform protected by crenellations. Occasionally a mural tower, square or rectangular in plan, might be set along the wall, but these were rare in the early period after the Conquest of England, and usually confined to weak spots in the circuit, such as covering angled turns.

The only tower on the wall might be the gate tower, approached across the ditch by a wooden causeway and often a drawbridge. It was soon realised that a gate in a wall needed additional protection, and in some cases this was afforded by placing a tower next to it as a guardian. From this the idea of placing the gate passage within the tower soon developed, running through it from front to rear, with access controlled by at least one door and possibly a portcullis. There might be one or more rooms over the passage, with wooden floors (at Newark there are two floors), within which would be housed any operating mechanism necessary for the portcullis, or perhaps for a drawbridge. Above that were the battlements. The side walls were sometimes drawn forward as deep buttresses to form a rudimentary barbican. Newark has a spiral stair enclosed in a turret at one corner. Compared to later gatehouses, with their huge flanking towers, machicolated battlements and multiple defences along the passage, these early examples are relatively simple. However, they might form the strongest part of an enclosure castle that was lacking a donjon.

The gate at Exeter, Devon, probably dates from the castle's foundation in 1068. It is now blocked up, but it is clear that the walls extended to form a primitive barbican. The arch is open behind.

Gate towers and gatehouses: Exeter and Richmond

Norman gatehouses varied in size and sophistication. Exeter's gatehouse (1) was built in the second half of the 11th century, its pointed Anglo-Saxon-style windows revealing its early date. Essentially it is a tower with a passage through it: the front walls extend forward, as can be seen in the plan view of the walls (2), and are provided with an arched top. Like the Tower of London, this castle, founded by William the Conqueror, utilised the Roman city defences to form two walls of the enclosure.

The 11th-century gate at Richmond, North Yorkshire (3), originally provided access to a large stone-walled enclosure above the River Swale (see plan view, 4). It was turned into a donjon in the mid-12th century when a stone tower was built on top and the original gate opening blocked by stone. A new, first-floor opening reached by timber stairs was added, leading to a single-roomed, two-storey interior over a blocked basement. The main living quarters appear to have been in Scolland's Hall at the other end of the bailey (5), so this donjon may have been the private solar tower of Duke Conan. It certainly demonstrated the lord's power, being the first impression gained of the castle from the town. There are three windows at first-floor level overlooking the town market place, one with a tympanum or filled stone space above the lintel: here the lord may have shown himself to the people via a wooden gallery. Similar arrangements survive at castles such as Newcastle and Dover, and early towers such as Oxford and Sherborne.

Castle Hedingham, probably built by Aubrey de Vere II in 1142. The forebuilding has been badly damaged.

Within the enclosure itself, the bailey was filled with all the buildings necessary for the inhabitants of the castle to subsist, especially if trapped inside the walls. The domestic buildings within Norman castles have not been studied to any great degree. On many sites later building has covered or destroyed the evidence, whilst on abandoned sites there has been relatively little exploration. Where this has been carried out, a picture emerges of a courtyard packed with all kinds of buildings, very different from the often half-empty castles depicted in artistic reconstructions until recently. Most were of timber, sometimes with stone footings to help protect the wood against rot, and many walls were constructed of wattle and daub. This process involved filling a timber frame, made from interlaced osier or willow twigs, with wattle. Each wattle panel was then daubed with a mixture of mud and dung, which set hard and formed a relatively insulated outside wall. A few buildings, such as two-storey halls, or sometimes the chapel, might be built of stone. Roofs were often of thatch, but some might be wooden shingle or slate. All castles would require a chapel, and if it were not in the donjon itself then a separate building would need to be built in the bailey. At Richmond the 11th-century chapel was located within the ground floor of a barrel-vaulted mural tower. Perhaps the most famous surviving chapel is the delightful, 12th-century circular example at Ludlow in Shropshire. It is decorated internally with arcading.

As with ring-works, some motte-and-bailey castles were adapted by replacing the timber palisades on the motte with stone, to form the so-called shell keep. Sometimes walls ran down the side of the motte to protect the stairway. Inside the walls on the summit, buildings of timber or stone could be butted against the walls. In a few instances a small tower was also added on top, the shell wall acting as a sort of chemise or skirt.

The castles that appeared in England immediately after 1066 usually lacked a stone donjon, the very building that many think of when a Norman castle is mentioned. The development of the donjon in England, and the use to which it was put, has been the subject of much recent debate. M.W. Thompson has promulgated a theory for the spread of such buildings in Britain.

One of the earliest stone towers in England is that of Chepstow in Gwent, which, it is generally agreed, was built before 1072 by the Conqueror's companion, William FitzOsbern. It stands on a cliff above the River Wye, a long rectangular building between two long baileys. One wall, on the cliff side, is little over 3ft thick, the others being 9.75ft. There is a decorated hall (with arched recesses) on the first floor. Thompson believes this building to be a *domicilium*, a first-floor hall of the type seen in France, with a thin wall one side but with a first-floor entrance, like a donjon.

The White Tower in the Tower of London is one of the earliest donjons in England, probably begun in 1077. It is of the type usually referred to as a 'hall keep', in which each main floor is divided internally by a cross wall to produce two rooms of unequal size. The cross wall also helps to reduce the span required for timber floor beams. The rooms are usually interpreted as forming a hall with an adjoining smaller chamber, though it is often difficult to prove whether they were actually used in this way. However, external access is always into the larger room. Sometimes further, smaller rooms are created by the addition of internal walls. The Tower took at least another 20 years to complete, at first apparently having the roofs visible above the parapet, and only being finished around 1102 by when the walls had been built up. There may well have been an intervening period of slow growth, since William Rufus, who succeeded his father the Conqueror in 1087, was more interested in the building of Westminster Hall, and it is more likely that the later spurt of activity at the Tower was due to his brother, Henry I (acceded in 1100). Similar to the Tower of London is the donjon at Colchester in Essex, which also possesses an apsidal, rounded corner. Unusually, it was constructed on the foundations of a Roman temple to the Emperor Claudius. It too is a very large building but not overly high, and it is commonly thought that the top floor has been destroyed, though this has been called into question.

It has been suggested these two donjons at the Tower and Colchester are based on the ducal example in Rouen, now vanished: as Thompson has pointed out, though, they are unlike the majority in France. Thompson's theory is that these donjons were a new concept in a relatively hostile land: the hall and separate chamber were placed side by side in a large tower adapted from the type usual on the Continent, often now classed as a 'solar tower', in which single rooms were stacked vertically. This provided a defended group of facilities under one roof. However, the tower at Ivry-la-Bataille in the Eure region of Normandy, which dates to about 1000, also has an internal dividing wall and apsidal corner, and may have been the inspiration for the brand new towers in England. Moreover, the defensive qualities of a castle as opposed to its symbolic role are now being questioned, and by the time these first hall keeps were completed there was little threat from the English, though baronial unrest was always a possibility.

The main floor at Castle Hedingham, showing the recessed window openings and the mural gallery.

So what were these new, great towers designed for? There is no record that William I ever visited the Tower of London, nor were the other Norman kings regular incumbents. Perhaps the rooms in the White Tower were designed for a kind of theatrical pageantry, whereby visitors were deliberately led through this hugely impressive stone building, their excitement increasing until they reached the king himself; perhaps only the most important guests were allowed to attain an audience in the upper chamber, the innermost sanctum of the monarch. This may have been the idea behind some of the larger donjons with their hall and adjoining chamber often duplicated on two floors, in which public and private rooms stood side by side, but since this rather neat division is a modern delineation it is more difficult to assess the role of these towers in contemporary eyes. Some public business might be conducted in the inner chamber, for example. Moreover, if a constable was in charge during the king's frequent absences, did he perhaps live within the lower chamber and hall? If little used by the monarch, a vast amount of work had gone into a project that then had slight value other than as a statement of great power, which may, of course, have been the main intention. If the king or lord of the place had his (perhaps temporary) residence there also, then so much the better.

Several early gate towers possess a large opening high up, rather like a door that opens on to nothing. It seems that these are located for the lord to stand and be seen by the populace, another theatrical display, this time in affirmation of his control over the area by his physical presence in his tower. One such opening appears in a gate tower at Sherborne, Dorset. The donjon built over the gate at Richmond, Yorkshire, has several openings that almost certainly led on to a wooden balcony looking towards the barbican and the town market place beyond. These deliberate and dramatic window displays did not last, though.

In some instances the lack of obvious accommodation within a donjon is so noticeable that the only conclusion to be drawn is that the tower in question was designed for little else but public function such as banquets or for a visitor

On one side of the cross wall at Castle Rising sits a kitchen on a stone vault; on the other side, seen here, there is a latrine through the left door and urinal through the right – perhaps separating the sexes?

to be received by the lord or king. A particular example is Castle Hedingham in Essex (*c*.1140), which has barrel-vaulted mural chambers so small that they could have served little purpose other than as store cupboards. Here too guests may have been led along a prescribed route ultimately to meet the Earl of Oxford.

Some early towers are quite puzzling. While several buildings in undefended sites are indisputably palaces, such as Clarendon, several examples within fortifications have thin walls and ground-floor entrances, though otherwise have the unequal internal division of a donjon. An example is Castle Acre in Norfolk, begun in the late-11th century by William de Warenne, Earl of Surrey, as a rectangular stone dwelling within earthworks. The walls were then thickened internally and during the 12th century the south side was demolished and the north side raised to make a tall donjon.

Many hall keeps survive in Britain and many suggest that, while not on the scale of palaces, they were residential, reinforcing the idea of the lord in his tower. Some 12th-century examples are quite refined when compared to the White Tower. Castle Rising has blind arcading carved along the external walls. As late as the 1180s, Henry II built the huge hall keep at Dover, by then a rather redundant building unless seen as an impressive statement of power and a royal residence. In the 12th century hall keeps were sometimes provided with a forebuilding, a rectangular stone building that butted against the main tower wall and masked the main entrance. Often stone stairs rose to the main entrance door and might be enclosed by the forebuilding. These stairs might be unroofed and open to the elements, to allow defenders to drop offensive material on any attacker using them: a few later examples were provided with arrow loops. However, the forebuilding also provided a stately entrance to the tower itself, as the visitor ascended to the main entrance doorway. The example at Dover was even provided with a stone bench that was centrally heated.

ABOVE LEFT The curtain at Eynesford, Kent, built *c*.1100, protected a timber tower with a mound built up around it. The flint-walled stone hall replaced the latter in the 12th century.

ABOVE RIGHT Corfe Castle, Dorset, *c*.1105, was slighted during the English Civil Wars. The cavity cut by sappers trying to demolish the donjons in 1646 can be seen at the bottom of the annexe, below the two latrine chutes.

This recumbent block of masonry at Corfe demonstrates the building technique of using ashlar facing with rubble filling behind.

Hall keeps remained popular, though towers comprising a simple set of single rooms one above the other were also built. The floors vary in number from three to six. One of the earliest examples is St Leonard's Tower at West Malling in Kent, built in the later-11th century by Gundulph, Bishop of Rochester, who also built the White Tower. It is enlivened on its external walls by a blind arcade of round-headed arches, and has four floors reached by a single corner spiral staircase. Another early tower is that at Oxford, which is slightly stepped. It may be this type of tower without a dividing wall that was the usual form in Normandy and in other areas of northern France, and therefore the ones at West Malling and Oxford too, are early examples of the style built by the Normans in their newly conquered land. The modern term 'solar tower' suggests that these formed private apartments for the lord while a larger hall (often now vanished) would have formed the main living area somewhere nearby. Notable later examples include the polygonal Orford (Suffolk), circular Conisbrough (Yorkshire) and the almost cruciform tower of c.1200 at Trim in County Meath, Ireland, where the visitor was guided through rooms to the lord. The number of mural rooms built into the designs often resulted in rather thin walls.

Compared to some hall keeps these solar towers are usually quite modest, with an internal area of between 36–100m². However, consideration must also be taken of how decorated such towers might be, regardless of size. Some have inadequate heating but are well-built and even decorated; perhaps such towers, provided with braziers, were used as sleeping quarters for family members or guests. Several towers, small and lacking refinements, give the impression they could have been little more than watch towers but even they would suggest to contemporaries that the holder had some wealth and status. There is evidence that solar towers may derive from wooden towers built on mottes or with mottes built up around them, as happened at several solar keeps. This, incidentally, may suggest the origin of the motte itself.

Donjons share many features, though not all display every characteristic. The main door is nearly always placed at first-floor level, reached by an external stair.

In many instances the latter may well have been of wood, capable of being destroyed if the entrance had to be protected in time of danger. Internally access between floors was usually by spiral vices set in the corner wall thickness, or occasionally by ladder and trapdoor. Few British donjons have straight stairs in the thickness of the wall. Some vices travel from basement to roof level, others occasionally miss alternate floors, forcing a detour across a room to reach a second stair to the next level, an obvious defensive advantage. Some corner buttresses are carried on up to form turrets. Additional buttresses are sometimes set against the wall face. Windows are usually small, sometimes being slightly larger on the upper floors, and occasionally of two-light construction. They are sometimes decorated with mouldings such as chevrons or billets. In many donjons the window opening splays into the room to maximise the light received. In some examples, however, a round-arched embrasure is set in the wall around the window. From these, or sometimes directly from the internal wall face, passages set in the thickness of the wall lead to small barrel-vaulted chambers or to privies. Some rooms are provided with round-arched fireplaces: those at the White Tower originally had hoods to help contain the smoke. From such fireplaces flues carried smoke out to openings usually set either side of a buttress. Where no fireplace exists, it must be assumed that heating was provided by portable braziers. Windows must have been provided with wooden shutters with drawbars, or in a few cases thin sheets of horn might be set in place. Some chapels may even have had glass in the windows, so rare it was probably removable to allow it to be carried on progress with its owner. A well was, of course, vital. Tales of defenders sucking the moisture from saddle leather, or drinking one another's urine or the blood of horses, illustrates the lengths men would go to in order to stay alive when the water ran out.

During the latter part of the 12th century, builders began experimenting with the shape of the donjon. A multi-angular design has several advantages. The angles, being shallower than the traditional right-angled corner, bonded the stones in more tightly and made it less easy to pick them out. On the battlements

Norwich Castle, Norfolk, was set on a motte but managed not to develop any cracks. Begun perhaps as early as 1095, it was completed in about 1115. The building was completely refaced in the 19th century, but carefully preserves the original lines.

there were no blind corners presented by the merlons that met at right angles, which forced a defender to poke his head out to see directly in front, thus presenting himself as a target. These advantages were obviously considered, leading to a variety of angular shapes, and to cylindrical towers. Odiham in Hampshire has buttresses attached to each of its eight angles; Orford has huge buttresses attached to its multi-angular sides; Conisbrough is cylindrical but is still provided with massive buttresses that break up the design. These buttresses actually add projecting angles to the design, and it is debatable therefore to precisely what extent defence was a consideration, underlined by the fact that rooms and passages were contrived in the wall thickness, thereby weakening it. Gradually cylindrical towers were built without buttresses, as in the late-12th- and early-13th-century donjons at Pembroke, Skenfrith or Tretower, the areas in the West Country and Wales where such donjons found favour, or, for example, at Barnard Castle in County Durham or Nenagh in Tipperary. The example at New Buckenham in Norfolk is apparently unique with a cross-wall, while Pembroke is actually provided with a stone dome rather than a timber roof, and has two concentric fighting galleries around it. A further advantage of such donjons is that they use less stone, though the circular interior feels less practical for domestic purposes. These polygonal and circular donjons may perhaps be seen as late forms of solar keep. Finally, the donjon was to be eclipsed by the strength of the outer defences, as the mural towers, hitherto relegated to a handful set at vulnerable points along the walls, or acting as gatehouses, were enlarged and multiplied in number. An early example of about 1180 is the splendid castle built by Roger Bigod, Earl of Norfolk, at Framlingham in Suffolk, which is distinguished by having no donjon: the defence relies solely on a strong line of towers set along the bailey walls.

Constructing stone castles

How were these castles erected? Perhaps surprisingly, little information was actually written down about the building of castles. Like any castle, a suitable site was first selected. We have already noted the use of existing Roman or Anglo-Saxon walls. Castles placed in towns might need buildings to be cleared before any construction work could begin, and this was done where necessary. At Lincoln, 166 houses were destroyed in 1068 to allow the castle to be erected where the Normans wanted it. Some castles were placed on angles of a river to command the route and use the protection of the water. Many were placed on natural hills, some on crags to benefit from the inaccessibility and from the solid rock base that deterred the use of mining. In the reign of William Rufus, for example, Robert de Bellême founded Bridgnorth in Shropshire on a hilltop site with a steep drop to deter assault, having abandoned his father's castle on the River Severn at Quatford. A rather nasty piece of work with an unhealthy interest in torture for the sake of it, he was nonetheless a fighting man with a sound knowledge of military matters.

Once the site had been selected, there might be a formal ceremony to announce the project. Building work then began, using specialist craftsmen, augmented by the toil of native Englishmen no doubt press-ganged into helping. The Anglo-Saxon demands of burgage work (i.e. on communal defences), together with the old obligation to man the walls, could be neatly turned into demands for such labour on castles or their repair, without too obviously contravening any customs. Once a castle was built work on it could become a traditional custom, or commuted for money. The construction of ditches was the work of diggers, who made them as V-shaped in cross-section, this providing for very steep sides that were sometimes revetted in timber. Some were designed to hold water and might be less steep. Timber bailey walls were laid on stone foundations.

The great donjons required the most planning, though. They were so immensely heavy that it was ill-advised to place them on an existing motte,

The donjon: Hedingham and Conisbrough

The exact purpose of the donjon or great tower has been the subject of much debate. A universal feature is that it demonstrated the power of the lord: though many could also provide a robust refuge, they were probably not designed primarily for this purpose. Some are likely to have served as private suites for the lord. The tower at Castle Hedingham, Essex (1), one of the best preserved, has recently been studied in detail. It has been demonstrated that the so-called top floor was simply roof space, the windows at that level being designed to enhance the building's grandeur when viewed from outside. The two main levels below, graced with beautiful Romanesque arches, had no provision for sleeping accommodation (the mural barrel-vaulted chambers are too small). The builder was probably Aubrey de Vere, who is likely to have erected the great tower to celebrate his elevation to the rank of Earl in 1142. The forebuilding (2) is now in a ruinous state; its precise form is uncertain.

The circular donjon at Conisbrough, Yorkshire (3), was one of the newer designs of tower in the late-12th century, but still possessed large buttresses. Internally it was provided with a single room on each floor and a vaulted basement; the main rooms had fireplaces and sinks. This was presumably a solar tower designed for the private use of the lord and his family. A hall and kitchen originally stood in the bailey, shown in the plan view (4). (A) is the keep, (B) is the gateway, and (C) the barbican.

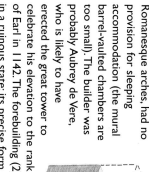

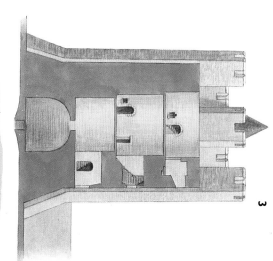

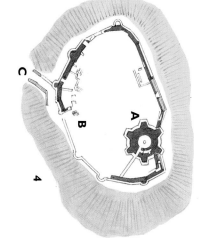

A corner stair in Norwich was converted into a kitchen oven, utilising the thick, solid stone of the wall to counter the risk of fire.

however small the tower might be, simply because a man-made structure had not settled enough to bear such a weight, and any further settling was liable to crack the masonry. A few donjons appear to have been built upon mottes, but on closer inspection it has been discovered that in fact the tower was placed on solid ground and a mound of earth built up around it to enclose and protect the base of the tower. At Guildford in Surrey an existing motte with shell wall has been used but only the eastern side of the motte has been employed so the donjon butts up on to it, being neither on it nor actually within it.

The building of donjons was in the hands of engineers, most of whom remain unknown. However, the Pipe Rolls of Henry II's reign contain the names of several of the king's masons. Alnoth the Engineer first appears in 1158 and worked for the king for 30 years; Maurice the Mason, while working at Dover, received a wage of 8d per day, putting him on equal footing with a knight (his pay later increased to one shilling). Maurice worked on the donjon at Newcastle before Dover, so it is perhaps not surprising that each castle bears some similarity to the other. Master Elyas of Oxford appears in 1187 in Oxford but worked in other places in southern England such as Portchester in 1192, and three years later is referred to as 'the Engineer' rather than stone-mason or carpenter. He had also been in charge of the royal siege engines from London for Richard I's siege of Nottingham in 1194.

Royal castles began life as an order passed as a king's writ to the sheriff of the county. Other sheriffs might become embroiled by way of demands for men, materials or transport. A royal official would act as the central authority, or else the designated constable. Royal quarries or those owned by monastic houses were large and might be hired as a whole or a designated amount of stone bought. Stone was cut by driving iron wedges to split away sections that were then sawn or further split by masons. One cubic foot was a common size for slabs, and their faces were often smoothed by chisels in a diagonal motion. Many castles were built using material from the nearest quarry, or even from the neighbourhood if the stone was usable. Hence, for example, the donjon at Goodrich in Herefordshire is of the same sandstone as the rock it stands on. The main method of transport otherwise was by water rather than road. It was by sea that some of the best stone, limestone from Caen in Normandy, was shipped to England to provide smooth ashlar facings. In England, Barnack in Northamptonshire, Maidstone in Kent (for Kentish ragstone) and Quarr were close to river facilities and provided good building stone. Sometimes Norman builders reused Roman red bricks, though occasionally they actually made their own bricks.

At the site the foundations preferred were those of solid rock, since this deterred mining, and once a level surface was cut, building could commence. However, where this was not possible foundations had to be created. A trench was dug slightly larger than the size of the walls, and filled with rammed stone rubble, or else oak piles driven into the soil by a weight and pulley system.

Occasionally an earlier building's foundations were commandeered, in which case a wooden raft was laid on top first.

The walls of a donjon were usually made by building a facing of ashlar blocks, and filling the gap with rougher stone, binding the whole together with mortar. Sometimes even builders' rubbish was used. When the great donjon in London was constructed it was rumoured that the blood of beasts was added to the mixture. Sometimes ties of metal or wood were added at intervals to help bond everything tightly. Not all castles had a smooth face, however. Some had the main walls built purely of rubble, in which case they had to be sheathed between wooden shuttering to allow the mortar to be poured and to set. Ashlar might be used at corners and around windows, to produce neat edging. As the walls of a donjon rose, square holes were left in them to allow beams to be inserted, which acted as supports for scaffolding. These putlog holes are still visible in Norman walls. On a few battlements such as Rochester, a line of holes below the crenellations indicates that the beams of wooden hoardings were fixed in them to overlook the wall base.

Many workmen would typically be employed on the building site of a major castle. Masons would be busy shaping blocks, men would burn lime and sand over fires to prepare mortar mixes, or melt lead brought from the Mendips or from Derby for roofing. Carpenters would be busy making or repairing items – the sheds to cover the craftsmen, scaffolding and floor beams, floorboards, window shutters, doors, or wooden shuttering for rubble walls or for door and window arches. Smiths would produce thousands of iron nails, hinges and handles. Tools had to be constantly resharpened. Sledges were used to pull heavy items, lighter loads being conveyed by stretcher or else in barrows or baskets.

Spiral stone vices were set into the walls using many wedge-shaped slabs of stone, each terminating at its narrow end in a circular slab, producing a sort of keyhole-shaped stone. The next step was laid on the top edge but the circular terminal was positioned over the first, like the centre point of a circle. Repeating this process formed the circular stair, whilst the stack of cylindrical slab-ends formed the vertical shaft or vice.

The remains of the north gate at Sherborne Old Castle, Dorset. Built between 1132 and 1137, this gate has a barbican formed from two long, parallel walls.

Once the main building was completed, the internal flooring could be added. Some castles were provided with a line of beam holes in the walls to take the floor beams; others used stone corbels (brackets) set in a line along the wall instead. The roof structure itself was usually of timber and was quite steeply angled. Wooden shingles, pottery tiles, slates or thatch covered the roof, or it might be coated in lead. Donjons with a spine wall were usually provided with two roofs, one to each room, and the top of the spine wall formed a natural gutter. Along the lower edges of the roof water runnels lined with wood or lead were usually cut through the thickness of the wall.

Waterpipes, drainpipes and spouts of lead were used. Doors were hung on iron butt-hinges. Wooden drawbars ran into holes in the adjoining wall, while two-leaved doors (i.e. with two halves) might have a pivoting bar attached. Some had locks as well. Work often stopped between Michaelmas and Easter unless it was a matter of urgency to carry on building, in which case it might also be continued at night. Expenditure on castles varied depending on their perceived importance. Henry II spent a hefty £1,144 on Newcastle upon Tyne between 1167 and 1178, but only £106 12s 9d on Norwich between 1160 and 1188 – less than was spent on Scarborough in one year (£107 6s 8d in 1160–61).

Tour of a castle: Dover

Of the numerous surviving Norman castles in Britain, one of the most impressive must be Dover. It combines a massive yet old-fashioned donjon with the most up-to-date concentric defences, barbicans and D-shaped towers, and incorporates work from 1066 to 1216 and beyond.

The castle at Dover is one of the largest in Britain. Perched on the heights above the town and looking out on the Straits of Dover, it occupies a strategic position of considerable importance. The site was not new, having been an Iron-Age hill fort, and already contained a Roman *pharos* or lighthouse and Saxon church when the Normans arrived. Some work, namely a bank and ditch to the south of the church, may have been carried out under King Harold as part of his alleged agreement with Duke William while on his visit in about 1064, but could also be part of William's work in 1066. The earthworks around the site ran well beyond the *pharos* and church, down to the cliffs that formed a natural barrier. The Normans concentrated on the upper, northern end, beyond the church. The earlier defences erected by the Conqueror, which are largely lost, were greatly improved upon by Henry II in the 1180s. In an area cut off from the rest of the complex by a ditch, he created an inner bailey surrounded by a towered curtain wall. Inside this space he built a huge hall keep, already rather outdated in style. All this work cost almost £6,300, an impressive sum. Beyond this area he began to construct an outer circuit of defences around the northern end of the site, beginning on the eastern side by the southern end of the inner walls, and running north-west on a similar axis. However, work was halted when he died in 1189, and was not taken up again until the reign of his son, King John. He spent over £1,000 between 1207 and 1214 on improving the defences and adding domestic buildings.

The huge donjon is one of the largest in the country, 83ft high, and 98ft by 96ft in area, with a battered plinth. The walls, of Kentish ragstone rubble with Caen ashlar dressings, are 21ft at their thickest, with a pilaster buttress in the centre of each side: spiral stair vices are set in the south and north corners. Around

The inner ward of Dover Castle, built from about 1170 by Maurice the Mason, for Henry II. The tops of the towers were later cut down and the battlements are missing. In front of the twin-towered gate the barbican has now been destroyed. Behind the walls looms Henry's great donjon.

the north-east and part of the south-east sides is a forebuilding providing stairs through three towers: the stairs (mostly modern, now with a right angle turn to the ground) were originally open to the sky to deny shelter to attackers (they were enclosed in the 15th century). The majority of rectangular windows are also reworkings of the 15th century. There seems to be an original doorway into the basement, an odd feature that would be a weak spot, though the door passage was defended by three doors with drawbars. The stairs rise to the lower chapel entrance in the first tower, with its porter's lodge (or perhaps a sacristy), then turn, and pass over a drawbridge pit to reach the second tower. Beyond is the third tower with guardroom, and to the left the decorated entrance doorway on to the second, or principal, floor. Leading from this passage is the vaulted well chamber with its shaft set in the thickness of the walls. It is lined with Caen stone for 172ft of its depth and additionally penetrates the chalk for 70ft or more. Only in the well chamber could water be drawn, to safeguard the supply if the basement was captured. From here two lead pipes, each 3.5in. across, carried water via wall conduits to the lower floors. The second floor was almost certainly the royal suite, divided by a cross-wall into great hall and chamber. The larger hall, entered from the stairs, has a door leading into the great chamber, where more exclusive audiences would be held. In the wall there are two mural chambers, one with latrine, perhaps the king's private bedroom. On the south side a passage connects the two rooms and leads also to a sacristy and second chapel in the forebuilding tower. Above the hall a mural passage runs right around the building, but is broken in the middle of the north-west wall, where it forms two ranges of back-to-back latrines with loops. Below, the first floor could only be reached by the spiral stairs. It is laid out rather like that above but with less elaborate decoration,

The donjon at Portchester was possibly built by Henry I. The date when the upper two floors were added is uncertain.

and the lower chapel can only be reached from the forebuilding. Below is the ground-level basement, with a narrow loop at each end of each room and a long mural storeroom in the south-west wall. The battlements are modern, and the flat roof was built in 1799; the original would have been much steeper in design. The vaults on the second floor were added at the same time, for carrying artillery pieces.

The inner bailey, built in the same material as the donjon, is set with 14 projecting square mural towers, with battered plinths all round the circuit: entrance is via a gate to the north (the King's Gateway) and another to the south (the Palace Gateway). Names given to various gates, it should be pointed out, are in many cases those of later constables and do not reflect the names (if any) used during the period under discussion. Each gate is flanked by two of the mural towers – the earliest such usage in Britain of a twin-towered gate. The gateways and drawbridges are of the 18th century. Each gate was protected by a barbican, but only the northern one survives, consisting of two walls forming a roughly triangular space, the path running at an angle to a gate with a segmental arch (an arch that is less than a semi-circle) offset from the main gate behind it. The barbican gate has a pit to accommodate a turning bridge. Each tower was originally taller and battlemented but has been much altered and refaced over large areas. It is open-backed. Inside the inner bailey

there was probably a kitchen in the south-east corner, and other domestic ranges against the curtain on these sides, now gone.

The outer walls were built by Henry II and John (later modified and cut down for artillery). From the south inner curtain a walled passage (now the 18th-century Bell Battery) ran east to the remains of Penchester Tower, before turning north. Here, on the eastern angle the northern and eastern ditches meet, possibly echoing an Iron Age entrance: Henry strengthened a potential weak spot at this point by constructing Avranches Tower – basically a two-storey polygonal firing platform, with three arrow loops on each face. This, together with double rows on the neighbouring stretch of curtain, enabled a withering fire to be concentrated on an enemy from over 50 arrow loops, together with missiles from the battlements. From Avranches Tower, Henry's curtain running north-west is set with two rectangular mural towers. It ceases just south of the FitzWilliam Gateway, Hubert de Burgh's work to add a postern in the 1220s. Also during Henry II's reign the ditch south of the church was filled in and a bank erected across it, then cut into for the foundation of a stone wall.

John did not initially concentrate much on Dover, and spent most on the castle after the loss of Normandy in 1204. He added domestic buildings inside the eastern side of the inner bailey, employed diggers to dig ditches and strengthened the outer curtain begun by his father, using new D-shaped mural towers in the latest design. On the northern point of the outer walls a new gatehouse with flanking towers was constructed, afterwards encased by Norfolk Towers following the damage caused by the siege of 1216, but still partially visible. The curtain running east to Henry's walls was also rebuilt following the siege. Running west and south from Norfolk Towers are Crevecoeur Tower (very cut down) and Godsfoe Tower, the latter rectangular, possibly having been used as a chamber tower to an adjacent hall, since there is a large blocked window

The base of the square tower at Farnham, Surrey, built c.1138, can be seen here on the left. It was protected by a motte, itself concealed behind walls raised in the late-12th century.

Dover Castle, Kent, early-13th century

Dover Castle in Kent was a huge and powerful fortress. This is a reconstruction of the castle as it probably looked during the reign of King John in the early-13th century, before the siege of 1216. The first concentric castle in Europe, the outer gatehouse (1) was provided with an earth and timber outwork or barbican (out of view at the bottom left); both would be damaged in the siege of 1216 and the gate blocked and rebuilt. The outer ring of curtain walls has arrow loops and internal embrasures (2). Some towers built by John are in the latest D-shape design (3), being curved where they face the field, while the one in the lower right (4) is polygonal. To its left, the square tower (5) may well be a chamber tower serving a hall complex behind it. The older mural towers on the far left of the outer ring (6 and 7) are the rectangular towers of Henry II, though beyond them at

the angle is Avranches Tower (8), shown also in closer detail (9), a tiered firing platform covering the re-entrant of the old earthworks. The inner circuit of walls (10) was built by Henry II, and consists of square mural towers, two of which form gatetowers to defend the northern entrance (11). This is itself defended by an offset stone barbican (12). Another similar gate and barbican lay on the south side (hidden). Within this circuit rises the great donjon (13), probably built to serve mainly as a royal residence and for receiving important guests. To the rear stands the old Anglo-Saxon church of St Mary (14) and the Roman *pharos* (15), in a low enclosure that Henry III would raise within great earthworks.

The original 11th-century gate at Richmond, Yorkshire, was blocked and turned into a donjon in the 12th century.

in the wall north of it. Moreover there is a well and latrine by the Crevecoeur Tower, suggesting domestic buildings in this part of the castle. Treasurer's Tower to the south is said to have been rebuilt by Edward IV in the 15th century. Beyond it, Constable's Gateway is the new gate Hubert de Burgh built in the 1220s to replace John's obviously vulnerable gate site on the northern tip of the outer defences. It incorporates one of John's D-shaped towers, seen behind the back-to-back D-towers forming Hubert's gate. Further south lies Queen Mary's Tower, the wall from here to Peverell's Gateway an 18th-century rebuild. Peverell's Gateway is a mural tower with spurred base backing on to a gateway, on the south side of which Henry III added a semi-circular tower. The brick parapet is of the 19th century. From here a section of (now vanished) walled passage ran via the destroyed Harcourt Tower to connect by the inner bailey near the southern gate (Palace Gateway), and thence along on the south side via the now destroyed Well Tower, Armourer's Tower and Arthur's Gate, which brings you to the south-eastern corner of the inner curtain, and to where the walled passage ran east to Penchester Gate. Thus the donjon was enclosed within two circuits of walls. Finally, a section of wall running along eastwards towards the church on this side ends in Colton's Gateway, which is also rectangular. The outer curtain to the south of the work of Henry II and John is largely that of Henry III's reign, and may have had palisades before this, but possibly only the Iron Age ditch and bank.

Beyond Penchester Tower the walls ran south-east along the line of the ditch, with two further towers, Godwin and Ashford, now completely lost. Whether they were the work of Henry II, John or Henry III is not known.

The principles of defence

All Norman castles offered protection for the garrison, but it should never be forgotten that these men were trained soldiers. Knights could be highly aggressive and were not averse to charging out on occasion to attack the enemy.

The first obstacle protecting any Norman castle was the ditch or moat surrounding the site. This was deep enough to make an effective obstacle, steep sided and perhaps revetted with wood to make it slippery to climb. It might be filled with stakes, not so much to impale the enemy but to slow him down and thus make him a better target. Some were flooded but most needed only a few feet of water and mud to present a real obstacle to easy movement. The earth was thrown up to form a bank on the inner lip, and often an outer bank as well. Stone bailey walls, though they rarely survive in any quantity, do not initially appear to have been too high. Those at Rochester have been estimated at about 22ft high and 4.5ft thick at the base. At Dover the inner walls of the 1180s that form the ring around the donjon have been robbed of their battlements. Framlingham looked to the walls and tall towers for its main defence.

Mural towers were fairly simple in design. Most were square or rectangular in plan, with two or three floors. Those on the strong inner curtain at Dover have latterly lost their fighting tops and been cut down to line up with the curtain wall. The towers at Framlingham were open backed, this closed by wooden screening or curtain. In time of war it meant the screens could be removed, exposing the inside of the tower and thus denying shelter to an enemy who managed to gain entry. Access across the tower at wall-walk level was by wooden planking, which could be thrown down if it appeared the tower might be lost. Each tower jutted out from the wall, and was provided with arrow loops in the side, to allow archers in the tower to enfilade the wall face or those on the battlements to shoot along the parapet below. By the 1180s a new concept was being tried out, whereby the tower was made multi-angled, then round, instead of square. The polygonal experiments gave way to towers either D-shaped, so they presented a rounded front to the field, or cylindrical. This allowed all round vison from the battlements, with no blind spots caused by angles, and provided no angles for a sapper's pickaxe to prize out stones.

At Framlingham the merlons were provided with vertical arrow loops with splayed backs. Some crenels could be protected by a wooden shutter, which pivoted on an iron bar: one end fitted into a hole in the side of a merlon, the other end into a short curved slot in the opposite end. They were presumably held open by a wooden peg, or simply lifted to allow an arrow or bolt to be loosed off.

Early gates were protected by a tower set beside them, but soon developed into the form of a square or rectangular tower pierced by a passageway. Above were one or more floors and battlements at roof level. It was late in the 12th century that a more substantial gatehouse appeared,

The roof level of the donjon at Richmond, with the battlements and the steps up to the corner turret.

now with twin square towers flanking a gate passage. This can be seen, for example, at Newark, whose massive recased plinths appear to be Norman, and at Dover in the inner and outer gates. Also new was the barbican or outwork, designed to help protect the gate, examples of which are rare. Sometimes these were of timber, as at Dover in the outer gate, here as late as 1216. However, the side walls of the late-11th-century gate at Exeter project slightly and are provided with an arch above, while at Sherborne in the 1130s a pair of parallel walls jutted forward down the bank from one of the gates. The barbicans protecting the north and south inner gates at Dover were of stone, the northern one of which survives as walls leading to a gate set off-centre from the main gate.

In the donjon itself defences were limited, and it is interesting to see how gradually these great towers fell from favour during the late-12th and early-13th centuries. The donjon at White Castle in Gwent was demolished when the castle underwent renovation, and defence was entrusted to strong round towers. The entrance was nearly always situated at first-floor level, being reached by a stair along the outside of the wall. This was often of wood, so that in an emergency, when everyone had retreated inside the tower, the stairs could be destroyed, presumably by burning, since it would take quite an effort to throw down a sturdy timber structure. Similarly, some stairs were interrupted by a drawbridge pit. This is seen, for example, in front of the forebuilding at Rochester, and in the approach stairs at Dover. However, it would be a hefty wooden platform that would be in use daily, and exactly how this was 'run back', as has often been written, is uncertain. Perhaps it had runners; perhaps it was simply burned away, or pushed off the edge of the entrance step by brute force.

The windows in a donjon were always quite small, though those on the upper levels might be slightly larger. Internally they were splayed to allow as much light

RIGHT **Defending a castle: Pembroke, Framlingham, and Farnham**

The main (and passive) defensive quality of a donjon was its solidity: when required, though, active defence was carried out from battlement level. In a few castles holes were created below the battlements for the erection of timber galleries called hoardings (1), onto which soldiers could step unseen beyond the crenellations. They could shoot through slits in the planking or command the base of the wall through gaps in the floor. The circular donjon at Pembroke (2), built by William Marshal in about 1200, is unusual in not only possessing these, but also having a second parapet and a stone dome, which obviously removed the danger of a timber roof being set alight or being smashed with missiles. The circular shape is seen in a number of late-12th-century towers, especially in the west. The removal of angles made it harder for enemy miners to pick out stones, and also removed blind spots from the corners of the battlements. The sloping battered plinth (3), seen on a number of donjons, thickened the wall base against attack and meant that material dropped from above bounced out at uncertain angles into the enemy.

The castle at Framlingham in Suffolk, built c.1180, had no donjon and relied for its defence on powerful curtain walls (4) set with rectangular towers (5). The towers were open-backed, fitted only with timber above battlement level and probably curtaining below that. The passage through each tower was spanned by wooden planking that could be removed, plus wooden doors; thus a section of curtain wall could be cut off if the enemy took it. The tower battlements were reached by ladder. The curtain walls were provided with embrasures each with twin vertical loops (6): the loops slope downwards externally, allowing plunging fire to the ground for archers. As these are now well above ground level, it seems they were reached from the first floor of a now vanished timber barrack block, though it is possible the ground level here has been lowered. On the battlements of towers and curtain wall, the merlon itself was sometimes provided with a vertical loop, internally splayed (7). Additionally, merlons were provided with a hole and slot to allow a wooden shutter to be inserted, to further protect archers on the parapet (8). The field-of-fire diagram shows the strength of the curtain walls and the fire cover provided (9).

The castle at Farnham, Surrey (10), may demonstrate the origin of the earth mound or motte. In about 1132 a square stone tower was built and its lower part enclosed in an earthen mound to protect it. However, in the later-12th century the tower was demolished until flush with the motte top, and a shell wall constructed at ground level to encase the motte (11). The gap between the wall and the curved top edge of the motte was later filled to produce a flattened surface. It may be, therefore, that mottes originated to protect the bases of timber towers in the same way.

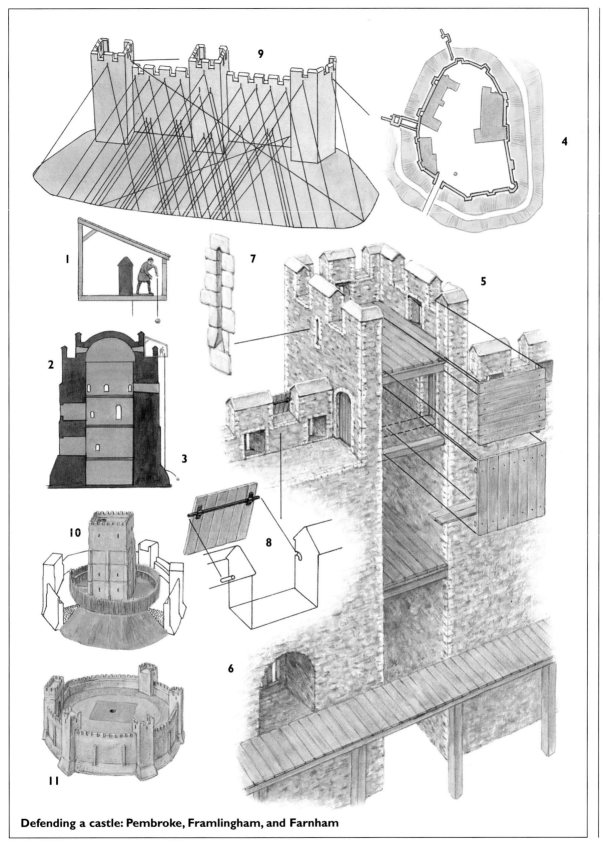

Defending a castle: Pembroke, Framlingham, and Farnham

Interior of the late-11th-century Scolland's Hall in Richmond Castle, looking west.

and air to enter the room as possible. It is often thought that some of these windows also served to shoot arrows from. However, a true arrow loop needs a plunging opening to the outside to allow the archer to shoot down towards ground level. Most of these windows do not possess them, moreover some are placed so high in a room as to make it impossible for an archer inside even to see the ground outside. Only a few, mostly late donjons possess true arrow loops, at a time when they are beginning to appear generally. They can be seen unusually early in Kenilworth (possibly c.1130), otherwise in late examples such as Skenfrith. Similarly, embrasures are built into the walls of Framlingham. The inside of the wall is cut out to form a cavity with an arched roof in the thickness of the wall behind the loophole. These are now several feet off the ground: presumably they were either reached by a platform, or else the ground level was higher than it is today. At Dover the early-13th-century Avranches Tower on the outer curtain wall is a good example of the new concept in defence, a mural tower with shallow angles rather than right angles, each facet set with three levels of arrow loops, which, with the battlements, allowed archers at three levels to pour missiles on to an approaching enemy and to command the ground below.

The base of many donjons is protected by a battered plinth. This is basically a thickening of stone at the base, angled like a flange to the base of the tower. It served two purposes: firstly, it strengthened the vulnerable base of the wall with additional masonry and secondly, it allowed any offensive material dropped from the wall head to bounce off the batter and fly into the enemy ranks at unpredictable angles. Such splayed bases were also seen on curtain walls and mural towers. By about 1200 some towers had spurs – thick, pointed masonry bases, jutting towards the field.

With arrow loops rare, and only the wall top to shoot from, defenders trapped in a donjon must have felt quite cut off: they would have to rely on the supplies stored in the ample basement and the water supply. Some internal staircases were staggered between floors, forcing anyone using them to cross the entire donjon to reach the next flight, but many did not have this refinement. Nor is it certain whether stairs spiralling upwards clockwise really were greatly beneficial to a right-handed defender backing up the stairs.

There are few references to donjons being besieged. The most famous concerns Rochester, besieged by John in 1215, when he brought down a whole corner by use of a mine. The defenders withdrew behind the massive cross-wall and continued to resist.

Some doors were guarded by a portcullis, now detectable in the vertical groove either side of the passage. Some were of wood shod with iron. Others, however, must have been purely of iron, as the groove is quite thin. At Rochester the door into the donjon from the forebuilding had a portcullis whose mechanism was situated in the entrance of the chapel above: the same applied to the main door at Orford, where its winch mechanism was also located, demonstrating the lack of concern this proximity presented to the military minds of the time. Doors were of thick planking, perhaps reinforced by metal. Drawbridges, lifted by means of chains and winches, are not detectable at the entrances to keeps, though Dover had one in the forebuilding, and a turning bridge at the barbican, which pivoted like a see-saw, the rear half falling into a pit as the front section was raised.

On the roof the battlements were usually raised up to a level that protected the roof from fire arrows or catapult stones. Here the main fighting platform was located, but on large donjons it might be 100ft or so above the ground. Some castles could erect wooden hoardings (brattices) out over the battlements, with the support beams using the holes provided under the battlements, thus allowing men stationed inside to command the foot of the wall below them whilst unseen from outside. However, though defenders might try and cover wooden hoardings with raw hides or clay, to snuff out flames, they were also vulnerable to catapult balls. Once inside a donjon, there was little chance of escape, since there would be no side door unless the tower was joined to a curtain wall, when there might be access to a wall-walk. In some castles there might be postern doors in the bailey.

Dover is one of the earliest examples of a concentric castle. The outer walls, built by Henry II on the north side of the complex, and added to by John, complement Henry's inner ring and, within that, his great rectangular donjon, hence a triple ring of defences. Here we see a slightly irregular concentric defence, not as refined as in later castles such as Beaumaris, where the outer ring runs almost parallel to the inner, but nevertheless an extremely early version of an inner wall supporting an outer. In theory this meant that the defenders possessed three rings of defence, the outer curtain, inner curtain, and donjon. However, the great donjon was already rather archaic in design. Here too we find early barbicans defending a gateway. Early Norman gatehouses basically consist of either a tower set beside a gateway set in a wall, or else a passage cut through the lower part of the tower itself.

Castles needed to have a water supply to hand. Some were supplied direct from underground streams and, like the White Tower in the Tower of London, the water was sourced via a well in the basement, so there was a supply on hand if the garrison was trapped in the donjon. At Rochester, the water could be drawn up through each floor by a shaft in the thickness of the cross-wall, a sort of watery dumb waiter. Dover had an elaborate piping system, whereby rainwater was

The mid-12th-century tower at Wolvesey Palace, Winchester, Hampshire, has provoked much debate. The walls are too thin to qualify it as a defensive tower, and it has been suggested this was a kitchen.

Carlisle Castle, Cumbria. The main walls and towers of this large castle were built by Henry I in 1122. The donjon, seen here, is attributed to the King of Scotland (1136–57) but may have been built between 1150 and 1175. The roof was later converted for use as a gun platform.

collected in a cistern and then fed via lead pipes. Sometimes water could be brought in by pipe from a river flowing past the castle. If there was no water under the donjon itself there needed to be a well in the bailey; but if defenders were forced into the tower with no water their only drink would be the wine or beer stocks stored there, before more unpleasant alternatives were considered out of desperation. Food supplies were also necessary and could be stockpiled in time of siege, since the basement of a donjon was usually spacious and must have been given over to storage. Many are subterranean or semi-subterranean, and few have any natural lighting. Some were reached by spiral stairs but others must have been accessed by trapdoor and ladder. Presumably there was a rope and pulley system for hauling up large items. Since few donjons possessed internal kitchens there would be little hot food if the defenders were forced inside the tower, other than that which could be cooked over the wall fireplaces or braziers.

The walls of Berkeley Castle enclose a motte. The manor was granted in 1153–56 and Henry II pledged to fortify a castle here.

Life in a Norman castle

As noted previously, the domestic buildings that filled the Norman castle have yet to be studied to any great degree. The hall was the largest building on the site. In Normandy halls were built in stone on two levels, with an undercroft on the ground floor in which food and drink were stored, and the main living area on the first floor, reached by an external stair. Anglo-Saxon and Danish halls, however, were built in timber with a single, ground-floor area of beaten earth. The roof of the hall was high-pitched, and running down its length on either side were a row of wooden pillars to help support the roof. The space between these and the outer walls provided an area for benches or beds, and spaces between pillars could be sectioned off as needed. A central hearth provided warmth, and a louvre in the roof helped remove the smoke.

Around the hall were satellite buildings. The kitchen contained at least one oven, probably with spits, tables for food preparation, shelves and hooks for storage and hanging utensils. At least one hearth was needed for large cauldrons for boiling ('seething') meat, a common form of cooking at the time. If the size of the castle warranted it, there might be a granary for grain and flour, probably set on short piles to guard against vermin. Otherwise dry food such as flour and bread would be kept in a pantry (the word deriving from the French word for bread, *pain*). The buttery (from the old French word *bouteul*, meaning bottle) held barrels of wine, beer and perhaps cider. Limited stocks of spirits, such as English mead or French brandy, might be held for the lord and his guests. Both these buildings would, from the late-12th century, be more frequently situated at the lower end of the hall, separated from it by the main entrance passage running across this end of the hall, the latter screened from the hall to shield against draughts.

The solar ('sun room') was the private withdrawing area for the lord, his family and guests. Anglo-Saxon and Viking social organisation had usually meant the lord and his followers all bedded down together in the great hall, and modern viewers would be shocked by the lack of privacy. By the time of

The latrine block at Wolvesey, showing the drainage channel.

the Norman Conquest this state of affairs may still have existed in some castles, perhaps amongst those lords inured to war and the comradeship it engendered. Many, however, were already seeking to distance themselves from the rest of the castle, at least for part of the day. Some so-called first-floor stone manor houses, such as Boothby Pagnall in Lincolnshire, are now considered by some to be in fact private solar blocks for a missing ground-floor hall. The solar would hold the lord's bed, a four-poster with curtains not only for added privacy – the whole family and guests might be in this room, as well as a body servant or two – but also to help keep out the draughts. Other furniture would include at least one large trunk or chest for clothes, and perhaps another for armour, though rods or rails for hanging clothes might be provided. A chair would be a luxury for the lord and lady. Stools, benches or the floor were good enough for most people. The floor might be covered with fur rugs. A favourite falcon or hawk might be kept on a perch in the room, and perhaps a favourite hunting dog or a lap dog for the lady. Inside a donjon or external hall the main rooms were probably plastered and perhaps whitewashed. Some could be decorated, a common theme being painted lines to represent masonry.

All castles would require a chapel, if not in the donjon itself then a separate building in the bailey. It might be anything from small and fairly plain to attractively decorated and impressive. The personnel varied according to the size of the structure and the importance of the holder. Some were set in the forebuilding, on the top floor or, in the case of Newcastle upon Tyne, its basement. Rochester is slightly unusual in having two chapels, one in the forebuilding and another on the top floor; however this was a bishop's castle. Orford's chapel is within a buttress and is small, plain and dignified, with the remains of a stone altar. The chapel at the Tower of London, though still exerting a quiet aura, has altered the south-east corner to include its apsidal end. The Chapel of St John has an arcade of pillars (as do several others such as the one in Durham Castle) supporting a barrel vault, and a gallery running around it. In the forebuilding at Dover the main chapel has a private entrance from the royal suite so the monarch could enter without passing through the main rooms. There also appears to be a lower chapel. Perhaps the most famous surviving chapel is the delightful, circular 12th-century example at Ludlow in Shropshire: internally the walls are decorated with blind arcading. A priest or clerk was required to provide religious teaching, to hear confession, to shrive the dying and to read and write a lord's letters.

Other buildings might include a brewery for producing beer, a bakehouse for making large quantities of bread, not to mention dovecotes to provide pigeons for the table. Barns contained fodder for animals, as well as farm equipment such as ploughs or harrows, for working the demesne in the nearby fields. They would also contain carts, in some royal or large castles quite a number, not just agricultural wagons but also the numerous vehicles required to carry all the equipment if the king or lord went on campaign or on a long journey. Stables were essential: not only were there knightly warhorses, but riding horses of varying quality, from good palfreys for the lord, lady and knights, to hacks for squires and perhaps mounted sergeants. Packhorses and carthorses were also needed. In some cases mules were used instead for riding, or as pack or draught animals, or oxen might be used to pull carts. All of these beasts of burden needed accommodation and food. Some lords might have kennels for a pack of hunting dogs, since hunting was almost an obsession with many Normans, not least the royal court circle. A large castle might even have a mews for keeping hunting birds.

Together with the housing for animals and equipment, there were the various workshops necessary for keeping a castle in working order. A carpenter's shop was essential since so much of even a stone castle was made from wood; the roof beams, flooring, doors and draw-bars, window shutters, some roof shingles, toilet covers, tables, benches, stools and chairs, shelves, cupboards, chests, beds, perhaps even shields and weapon staves, not to mention those domestic

buildings constructed from wood. Together with this work went that of the blacksmith: he provided nails for everything, as well as hinges, door handles and bolts, iron implements of all sorts, plough shares, etc. In many castles he may have turned his hand to repairing or making simpler pieces of armour, but this was more the job of the professional armourer or mail maker, who might also produce, repair or sharpen weapons. Smiths would need a furnace, bellows, anvil and water trough or bucket for quenching. Their workshops would need to have either shuttered windows or none at all, to allow them to judge by colour when to remove metal from the fire.

The size of population living in a castle varied greatly. Royal castles might only see the king occasionally and therefore be run on a skeleton staff. Some lords of modest means simply could not afford a large staff. The lord had to maintain the fabric, to make sure the garrison was at its correct strength and that those liable to perform service did so at the required time and for the required period. Noble youths sent from the households of other lords were under his tutelage and were assigned to knights for training as pages or squires. He and his lady also toured the estates held by them, to check with their stewards on the produce being farmed. The lady of the castle also usually oversaw the domestic routine of the castle, including the daily menu and the ordering of supplies. It was routinely her task to oversee the reception and entertainment of guests. A lady might well have a number of ladies-in-waiting, themselves sometimes the wives or sisters of knights, and families were often quite large, with numerous sons and daughters. Babies required wet nurses or ordinary nurses to look after them. The lady was ultimately responsible for the training of girls from noble households who were learning to be ladies. She nominally ran the castle if her lord was absent, or indeed if she were a widow. This might well include supervising its defence during a siege.

ABOVE LEFT The rear of Orford Castle, built c.1165, showing the group of vents for the latrine chutes at the bottom of the wall.

ABOVE RIGHT The altar still survives in the chapel built in one of the buttresses at Orford.

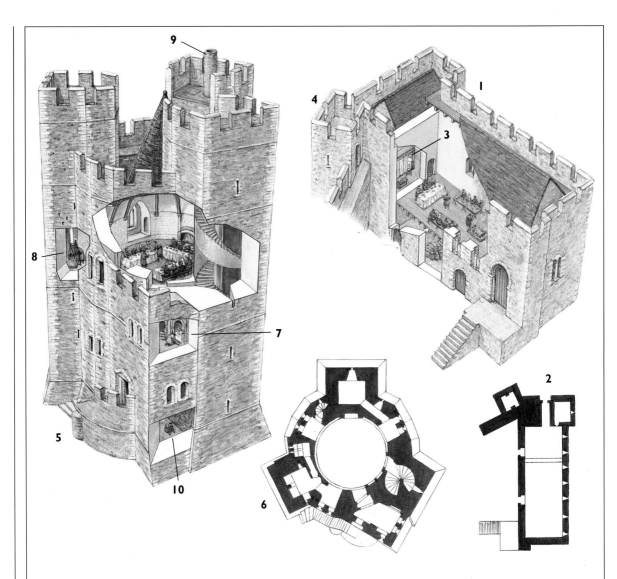

The living castle: Richmond and Orford

In many castles the main living area was a hall in the bailey, whether or not there was a donjon. Scolland's Hall in Richmond Castle, North Yorkshire (1, also shown in ground-floor plan view, 2), was built in the late-11th century before the gate was transformed into a donjon in the mid-12th century. It is a first-floor hall set on an undercroft that led at its eastern end out into a barbican. On the first floor (reached by an external stone stair) this eastern end was divided off to form a withdrawing room or solar for the lord and his family (3). At the north corner was a small tower that contained the latrines (4). Cooking was carried out in a separate building outside. It was not until the 13th century that the hall was redesigned in the latest style by adding a kitchen flanked by pantry and buttery at the western end: the kitchen was reached by knocking the window through to form a doorway.

Orford in Suffolk (5), built by Henry II in about 1165, has a polygonal tower in the new experimental style. However, the large buttresses give it even squarer angles, as well as blind spots, while the numerous rooms set in the buttresses mean the walls are quite thin (see the entrance-level plan view, 6). This all suggests the tower was not designed primarily for defence. As a solar tower, however, it does contain all the conveniences for a king and his guests. There is a small chapel (7), a kitchen with fireplaces, a sink and drain on each of the two principal floors (8), garderobes, a urinal outside one of the mural chambers, and a bread oven in one of the roof turrets (9). A chamber below the entrance with a narrow entrance from above may be a prison rather than a store (10), due to the inconvenient entry. It has also been suggested that the dimensions of the building, like those of cathedrals, have symbolic meaning.

Kings and great lords held a number of castles and were in any case often on the road, overseeing royal or feudal justice, attending courts, meeting with peers or vassals, visiting estates or towns, or travelling with an army. When such men were absent (and some fortresses might rarely see their lords) a castle was held by a representative, the constable or castellan, who basically carried out his master's duties for him. Crucially, if the castle was liable to be attacked he must know what his master's intention would be, and if not, then find out. It would not do to surrender to an enemy if his lord had expressly forbidden it.

The most important contingent of a castle's inhabitants was its fighting men. The knights and sergeants who formed its garrison were, in the years immediately following the Conquest, often household men brought in with the lord who lived in the castle and were ready for instant action. Increasingly, as the country settled down, knights were given portions of land to settle and in return performed service. At the time of King Stephen this seems to be have been two months per year in time of war and usually 40 days in time of peace. This latter service could be basically broken down into two parts, castle guard and escort duty. Castle guard was performed at one or more of a lord's castles. Thus castles were defended by a rota of a lord's men, serving as garrison soldiers. This service, useful after the Conquest, meant that large numbers of men were called up for duty when not really needed in time of peace, and it became more difficult to enforce castle-guard service. From the time of Henry II lords began to bargain with tenants to enable them to commute the service for money, as much as the lord could squeeze from them, though usually not enough to hire a substitute. With this he could employ smaller garrisons of mercenaries, topped up by feudal troops in time of war. Gradually it became more difficult to enforce such service, which fell into decay when feudalism itself declined. King John was notorious for employing large numbers of foreign crossbowmen, something that helped alienate the weapon in England. In time of war the size of a garrison might alter as feudal fee holders were called in to reinforce a garrison or to form part of a larger body of men using the castle

A fireplace and sink in a kitchen set within a buttress at Orford.

The triangular urinal in the wall passage outside a mural chamber at Orford.

as a barracks whilst awaiting orders to move out on campaign. Equally castles in Marcher areas needed men to be ready for action.

Other people might live in a castle, and their numbers varied depending on the size and importance of the fortress. A seneschal or a steward might look after the household, taking orders directly from the lord or lady. A marshal might see to the defences and the training and equipment for the soldiers. He also had responsibility for the horses, for buying or selling as necessary, and to direct the grooms who tended the beasts. A butler might be employed to run the kitchens and would be responsible for supplies of wine and beer. At least one cook was needed, with kitchen servants to assist and servers to take the dishes to the tables. In royal castles entertainment might be lavish: King John ordered ovens to be built at Marlborough and Ludgershall large enough to take two or three oxen. Castles were also places for celebrations. Indeed, it appears that the donjon at Hedingham in Essex was designed largely to mark the elevation of John de Vere to the earldom of Oxford. The hall of a castle was large enough to hold gatherings, and it was normal for kitchens to be a short way from the hall, whether in manor or fortress, so folk were probably used to barely-warm food. Kitchens sited in the bailey would be of a suitable size to accommodate the amounts of cooked food required. Only in smaller donjons, where a limited clientele was to be catered for, might a kitchen be sited inside the tower itself. Thus Norwich has a kitchen oven added into the corner where a stairwell once stood. Castle Rising in Norfolk has a kitchen on a stone-vaulted floor at one end of the donjon, with what appears to be a pantry next door complete with cupboard areas formed in the stonework, all cut off by partition walls. The circular tower of Conisbrough in Yorkshire has a sink channel set in the wall on two floors, while perhaps the most perfect en suite facilities are to be found in Orford, the famous polygonal donjon built by Henry II in about 1165. Here the great buttress on one side is used to accommodate fireplaces (where the stone floor helps protect against fire) and sinks, though it has been suggested that one of these is a bath drain.

A few castles also boast the occasional urinal, a rare utility in a Norman donjon. Privies are much more common in donjons, set within mural chambers reached by a short passage or sometimes without one. They are sometimes formed in pairs, side by side or back to back either side of a wall section, and thus sometimes share a chute. Some are obviously designed for use by anyone in the main room, but others lead from a mural chamber and are obviously more private. Some were provided with a wooden door, probably more to block off odours than for privacy. Window openings in a privy might well have no shutter, the better to vent the room. The opening of a privy would be covered by a wooden seat, probably with a rectangular or keyhole aperture cut in it. The waste passed out through an opening on the outside of the wall face, some of these being quite elaborate: Castle Rising boasts tall arches covering the vents. If there was a convenient nearby river or moat the waste could fall into the water, but often it simply rolled down to the foot of the wall and would eventually (presumably) be removed by a dung farmer. Dover has a cess pit at the bottom of one wall with a small archway in a central buttress giving access; but the ordure still sat there until dealt with.

Servants were necessary to tend the daily needs of the richer members of the castle community. Washerwomen and serving girls would also be seen. For the lord's pleasure falconers took care of his birds and dog-keepers cared for the hunting dogs sometimes housed in kennels within a castle. Such people might well travel with the lord as he moved about the country.

In time of war, if a castle was besieged, it was the garrison's duty to bear the brunt of the fighting. However, all hands might be called upon to assist in its defence, even if it only meant hurling stones from the battlements or helping tip a pan of boiling water over the heads of attackers. If the walls were breached, the enemy would think little of butchering anyone they found inside, and would delight in raping women or girls. Thus a spirited defence was advisable.

Castles were, of course, centres for controlling the surrounding area. Since armoured knights could comfortably ride out perhaps ten miles or more and back in a day, each castle effectively controlled the area within a radius of at least ten miles. In times of unrest, notably in Stephen's reign, castles could become a real liability. If their holders defied royal authority the troops within could become a menace to the surrounding area. However, the famous anarchy of Stephen's reign, 'when Christ and his saints slept' as one chronicler put it, has been exaggerated and, moreover, was not widespread over the whole country. The notion of the robber baron, seizing innocent victims to torture in his dungeons to reveal their wealth, is rather overdone. No doubt it did happen on occasion, and no doubt a castle was sometimes viewed by those outside with suspicion, but it was still a part of the scene. It was not simply an imposing set of barracks for housing men. Often a lord would use the most important of his fortresses, the 'chief' of his honour, as the centre for his court and, following from that, the centre for the administration of his estates. If a nobleman had been appointed high sheriff of a county, the castle within the

The interior of the circular, free-standing chapel at Ludlow Castle, Shropshire, probably built in the mid-12th century.

Scarborough, Yorkshire; the castle walls and tower were built between 1127 and 1177. The donjon, shown here, dates from between 1157 and 1169, though.

main town was usually the seat of his power. Together with administration came the dispensation of justice. By the time of Richard I judges were sent round the country to hear cases and represent the king. For a lord in his castle justice meant hearing complaints in the manorial court, but it was also the scene for feudal courts to deal with matters of honourial dispute between vassals or tenants. A castle was a convenient place to hold suspects, perhaps those caught poaching deer, but they were not generally designed for use as prisons, and men were held until a hearing was arranged, when the king, sheriff, judge or lord, depending on the case, was in the area. Once a case had been heard, a person found guilty was punished by fine, mutilation or execution. Usually only in church courts was imprisonment imposed as a punishment, though those captured in battle, either awaiting ransom or royal justice, would usually be penned up.

Siege warfare

Numerous Norman castles were besieged in the period from the Conquest to the death of King John. Some sieges were very swift, lasting but a few days. Others, mainly those of important strongholds, dragged on for two or three months. There were several periods when siege warfare was marked in England. The first was during the turbulent period directly after the Norman Conquest, but much of this was against towns and cities held largely by Anglo-Danish inhabitants, such as Exeter which was taken when William drove a mine under the walls, or York which he visited three times in three years. Their defences comprised surviving Roman and Saxon works, and fall outside the scope of this book. The second period was during the civil wars of Stephen's reign. A number of these sieges were also against towns, or against earth and timber castles. In 1173–74 came the determined attack from Scotland on the north of England, resulting in numerous sieges. Finally, civil war broke out in 1215 against King John, only ending with his death the following year. This last period saw the greatest set-piece sieges of the time.

During the civil wars of Stephen's reign, the king learned that the Empress Matilda had taken refuge in Oxford Castle. The royalist troops arrived on the banks of the River Thames in September 1142 to find the Angevin garrison on the other side manning the battlements and shooting arrows at them across the river. Wasting no time, Stephen moved to a fording place in the river that nevertheless required swimming, and plunged in to lead his men across. Angevin soldiers outside the gates were pushed back as the royalist troops surged forward. They forced the gates of the city and charged in, torching the houses and setting fire to the city. Then, arriving in front of the castle, they settled down to a siege. Matilda was trapped.

Oxford Castle was considered a tough nut to crack. It comprises an oval enclosure, ditched and banked, beside the river. This was originally topped with stone curtain walls rather than palisades. On the far side stands a motte: it was partly cased in clay to prevent slippage, and topped with two decagonal shell walls, some 58ft and 22ft in diameter. Simple square towers were set along

Battlement level at Rochester Castle.

The interior of the donjon at Rochester of c.1130, showing the arcaded spine wall on the left incorporating the well shaft with its access doorway.

the curtain, one of which, the stepped St George's Tower, may be the 'very tall tower' mentioned in the *Gesta Stephani*. It is built of coursed limestone rubble with a diagonally set stair turret.

Stephen built a siege-work to the north of the castle, and settled down to wait for the defenders to starve. He posted sentries all around to prevent escape, and then brought up siege engines, more to lower morale than to effect a breach. Brian FitzCount organised a force at Wallingford to try and rescue the Empress, but refused to attack the royalist siege lines. Robert of Gloucester threatened Wareham, allowing the commander to send a message to Stephen that he would surrender if the king did not come to their aid within a certain time. He hoped this would draw Stephen away from Oxford, but Stephen obstinately refused to leave. Meanwhile Wareham surrendered and Robert went on to capture Portland and Lulworth castles.

Just before Christmas, one of the most famous incidents in siege warfare occurred. Supplies were running low in Oxford Castle, and the Angevins inside were getting desperate. It was cold: deep snow covered the ground and the Thames was now frozen over. One night Matilda, covered in a white sheet for camouflage, succeeded in slipping out of the castle and away. She may have shinned down a rope or simply crept out of a postern gate, the latter being the more likely suggestion of William of Malmesbury. The sentries were evidently not asleep, for we are told there were trumpet calls and shouts, but nobody spotted her as she crossed the ice with three or four knights to escort her, and made her escape to Abingdon. At Oxford the garrison now surrendered and were treated honourably by the king. It is interesting to note that Oxford Castle, considered strong enough with its walls and towers, was not even assaulted by Stephen, who was content to endure a long siege to starve out his prey, even though the winter conditions would be horrible for his own men. There was no large donjon to intimidate the besiegers with a show of impregnability, and St George's Tower, while strong, is not an especially large building by comparison to others.

Interesting details of siege warfare against castles with stone defences and donjons emerge during the Scottish invasion of England in 1173–74. King William of Scotland came south to claim back Northumbria with a powerful army that included many Flemish mercenaries, and in so doing laid siege to a number of castles in the north of England. In 1174 his troops spent three months besieging the strong fortress of Carlisle in Cumbria. The castle is triangular in shape, with a donjon in the inner bailey in the eastern corner, and a large outer bailey. The donjon was erected by about 1175 and the Scots threatened to throw the castellan, Robert de Vaux, from the top of the tower if they captured him. Carlisle did not fall, and when the Scots tried to bribe de Vaux instead with gold and silver, he replied that the garrison was loyal to him and that they had plenty of wheat and wine. In the event the besiegers finally withdrew on hearing of the capture of King William at Alnwick in Northumberland. Before this, while some of his troops were at Carlisle, William himself had marched on Appleby in

Westmorland, a modest castle with a small donjon and which, the chronicler Jordan Fantosme states, was undefended and offered no resistance at all. Its elderly constable was later fined a hefty 500 marks by Henry II for his dismal performance. The Scots then occupied the donjon in high spirits.

The Scottish army then attacked Brough Castle in Cumbria, which was defended by six knights. Brough was basically an enclosure defended by walls erected in about 1100, with a square donjon at one end, against which the curtain terminated. The Scots laid siege to the castle on all sides and, after a hard fight, they managed to take possession of the outer walls the same day. The defenders pulled back and sought refuge in the tower. Temporarily foiled, the Scots brought up combustibles and set fire to the tower. This would suggest it was made of wood, but the foundations of that tower survive, showing it was of stone, built on the remains of Roman barracks, with a huge foundation of herringbone masonry. As the fire and smoke took hold, the garrison surrendered, and all appeared to be over. However, as Jordan relates, a newly arrived knight would have none of it. Remaining in the donjon he took two shields, climbed to the roof and hung them over the battlements. He threw three javelins down on the Scots, killing a man with each. Then he seized sharp stakes and hurled them, shouting 'You shall all be vanquished!' Once the shields had been consumed by fire, he decided he had done enough and surrendered. Jordan relates that 'the better part of the tower' was overthrown, suggesting that after the siege the Flemish soldiers assisted in its demise with pickaxes. Once again a donjon had revealed its weakness. The respite for the hard-pressed garrison had been only temporary. The enemy had not gone away but continued with their efforts to take the whole castle, successfully in this case. Only from the battlements could the defenders fight back. Nevertheless, in the late-12th or early-13th century a second stone tower was erected on the foundations of the first at Brough, set on a raft of timbers, which survives to this day. Clearly it was felt that these donjons were still worth erecting.

After a blooding while attempting to seize the motte and bailey at Wark, the Scots moved on to Prudhoe. This was a walled enclosure with a square stone gatehouse, and a small donjon at one end, complete with forebuilding. Its lord, Odinel, rode out on hearing of King William's demand for surrender, leaving a determined garrison while he reluctantly went off in search of additional troops. When the Scots arrived they tried to assault the outer walls but the garrison stood its ground and beat off all attempts. The besiegers nonetheless did much damage to the surrounding land and gardens, destroying crops. Finally, King William decided to withdraw from the siege, and the castle was never taken. However, in a reversal of political fortune, Prudhoe surrendered to King John in 1212.

The siege of Rochester in 1215 is one of the great set-piece sieges of a donjon in Britain. King John had encountered problems concerning who should hold

Castle Rising, Norfolk, was built by William de Albini in the late-1130s, based on Norwich. The forebuilding has stately decoration.

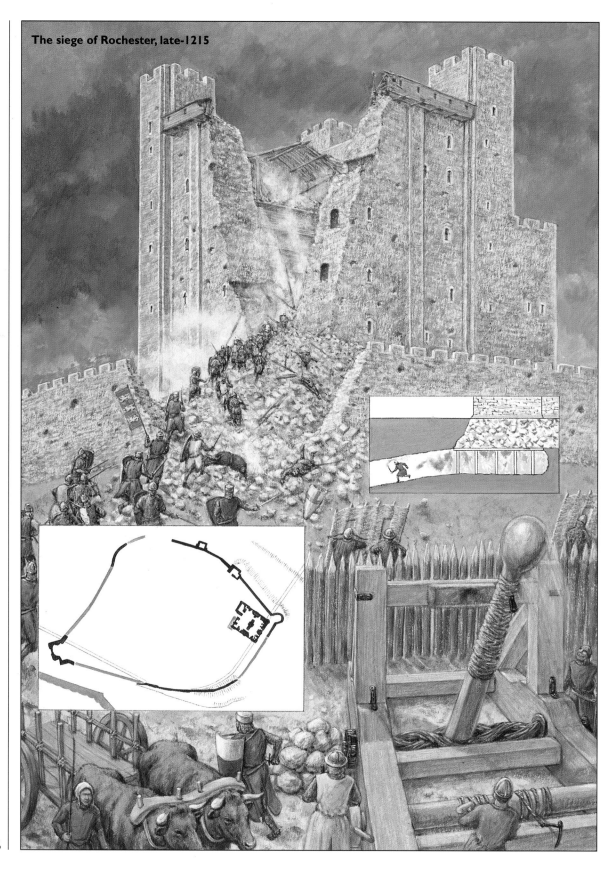

The siege of Rochester, late-1215

46

the castle, namely the Archbishop of Canterbury or a constable. After John's agreement to and, soon afterwards, repudiation of Magna Carta in June 1215, Rochester was restored to Archbishop Stephen Langton, but in August letters patent transferred it to a friend of the king, Peter des Roches, Archbishop of Winchester. At the end of September a group of rebels entered the castle and said they were holding it with the consent of its constable, Reginald de Cornhill. This move helped block the route to London, where the rebels had their headquarters, since John was at Dover. The rebel leader, William de Albini, realised that the castle was low on supplies and did his best to provision it. The garrison appears to have consisted of sergeants, crossbowmen and others, a total of between 95 and 140 men.

Unfortunately for William, John wasted no time in confronting him. The king had been busy recruiting mercenaries but already it seems some of his troops had arrived at Rochester from the direction of Malling. The royalists massed on the banks of the River Medway and the bridge over it was broken down to stop any advance by relief forces from London. Ralph of Coggeshall says the first royalist attack on the bridge was beaten off but the king's men persisted and on 11 October managed to enter the city itself in a surprise attack. The castle was now put under siege, and John himself now appeared on Monday, 13 October.

The king probably set up his camp on Boley Hill, and lost no time in erecting five catapults to harass the defenders. The bombardment became a relentless pounding both day and night, backed up by missiles from archers and cross-bowmen, one contingent relieving another to keep up the pressure. Those inside reciprocated with vigour, their crossbowmen inflicting a number of casualties. At one point (according to a possibly apocryphal report) a crossbowman noticed that King John, busily inspecting the castle for weak spots, had come within range, and asked William de Albini for permission to shoot. The reply came that it was not up to ordinary people to kill God's anointed, and John passed unscathed. The limited time that the rebels had enjoyed to prepare for the siege began to be felt, as provisions ran dangerously low; men resorted to eating horseflesh, even their precious war horses, and drank water, both of which activities, we are told, were quite alien to men of rank. Roger of Wendover says that the catapults actually achieved very little, apart from being a nuisance, but the Barnwell chronicler recounts that the engines finally breached the walls of the bailey. However, Wendover attributes this to the work of miners, who dug a tunnel under the walls and brought down a section of the defences. A writ dated 14 October demands

The impressive entrance stairs to first-floor level within the forebuilding at Castle Rising.

LEFT The siege of Rochester, late-1215

King John besieged the rebels in Rochester on 11 October 1215. His assault began by breaching the curtain wall (see inset plan view), probably by means of a mine though one chronicler says catapults were used (a torsion catapult can be seen in the lower right of the illustration). However, the great donjon was impervious to such missiles and the sappers set to work to undermine the corner. When work was done, the props in the tunnel were set alight (see inset); pig's fat was used for fuel. Having burned through, the mine collapsed and brought the entire corner section down. The main illustration shows royalist troops surging forward, as the defenders withdraw behind the cross-wall of the donjon. Here they continued to resist, until starvation forced them to surrender. Note the timber hoardings on the battlements and the large forebuilding on the right-hand side of the castle, guarding the entrance.

that the reeve of Canterbury oversee the manufacture of as many picks as possible, to be sent speedily to the king. A possible mining trench has been discovered north of the most northerly of the two mural towers on the east side of the castle.

On 26 October rebel leaders in London approached with a relief force of 700 cavalry but changed their minds on reaching Dartford, probably because John was marching to meet them and, says the Barnwell chronicler, they lacked foot soldiers.

As the bailey wall was breached, the rebels inside the castle retired into the massive bulk of the donjon. It was safe from catapults but not safe from the king. John now ordered a mine to be dug under the south-east corner, the only option left to him – short of starvation – that might result in the castle's capture. On 25 November he despatched a writ to his justiciar, Hubert de Burgh, with instructions 'to send to us with all speed by day and night forty of the fattest pigs of the sort least good for eating to bring fire beneath the tower'. With the mine dug and shored up with wooden props, and wood piled below the stone seating, the whole was smeared with pig fat and set alight. As the fire increased and the props burned away, the gaping hole left by the miners below the angle took its toll. With nothing to hold it up, the corner cracked and collapsed, exposing the inside of the donjon itself.

Yet the defenders still defied the king, now withdrawing behind the cross-wall to continue their resistance. Although the attackers could command the south-west of the two main rooms, their only access through the cross-wall on the ground and first floor was via two narrow doorways, easily defended and probably barred. Presumably the defenders did not attempt to hold the principal floor above, since here the cross-wall was represented by arches. Moreover, the corner stair well was now in the hands of the royalists, who could use the gallery running round the principal level. Here too they could access the stair in the opposite corner and descend to emerge into the room held by the rebels. We do not know if this was tried, whether any struggles took place as John's men attempted to force a way from the stair doorways. What is known is that the garrison was not beaten by direct assault, but by failing supplies of food and water.

Still hopeful of a relief force, the rebels refused to lose heart. The first casualties were those of least value, pushed out to be seized by the royalists, who it is said cut off the hands and feet of many. Soon, inevitably, the rest were captured, and the castle passed into John's hands on 30 November. John, in a fury, was all for hanging every one of the nobles taken, and since the castle was taken by force he was quite within his right to do so. However, Savaric de Mauléon, a royalist captain, managed to sway him from this course of action, since, he pointed out, it would cause retaliations against royalist garrisons in the same position and cause them to surrender to avoid a similar fate. In the event, John hung only a crossbowman turned traitor whom he had taken care of since boyhood, while most of the men of rank were packed off to Corfe and other royal castles for safekeeping. John left with much of his army but on 8 December sent a writ from Malling ordering money for his half-brother, William Longespée, Earl of Salisbury, so that he might leave Rochester with suitable honour. The damaged donjon was still considered important and was rebuilt with a rounded corner in Poitevin style, which remains to this day.

The siege shows the strengths and weaknesses of the donjon. Once the bailey wall had been breached, the defenders, faced with a powerful royalist army, had no option but to take refuge in the great tower, but here they could do little to fight back. Though very difficult to damage significantly with missiles, the donjon was, like any castle wall, vulnerable to the deadly mine. Whether the defenders could have held out beyond the cross-wall if provisions had been sufficient is debatable. The siege was the greatest to date in England: the Barnwell chronicler makes the telling comment that 'after it few cared to put their trust in castles'. An interesting footnote is that the following year Prince Louis of France, the new rebel leader, arrived before Rochester and took the castle: unfortunately no details of how this was done have survived. At Easter 1264 the castle was again attacked and again the defenders (royalists of Henry III this time) withdrew into the donjon. Various reports mention a mine and bombardment but the tower was never taken because the siege was raised in two weeks.

Not long after Prince Louis attacked Rochester he launched a major assault against another tough castle, this time at Dover. Having landed in Thanet, Kent, in May, Louis had caught John by surprise, and the king just had time to provision Dover and place the justiciar, Hubert de Burgh, inside it, supported by 140 knights, while he rode for Winchester. In the autumn Louis settled himself in Dover Priory to direct the siege, setting his camp north-east of the castle itself. The French saw that the castle lay below the crest of the hill, and resolved to use it to their advantage. They fixed their efforts on the main northern outer gate, newly built by John. In front was a ditched outwork or barbican, but its walls were of timber, presumably a late attempt by the royalists to defend the gate. Amongst other engines placed in the besiegers' camp was a great *petrarie*, or stone-thrower (probably a counterweight trebuchet), nicknamed *Malvoisin* ('Bad Neighbour'), which pounded the walls. A huge siege tower or belfry was begun, protected by hurdles and with a covered bridge to stretch on to the battlements of the wall tops. Meanwhile miners quietly began to undermine the outwork. During this time the energetic garrison made several sorties to damage engines or kill enemy troops. However, the French miners did their work: the outwork was under-

The donjon at Newcastle upon Tyne was probably built between 1168 and 1178. The battlements have been rebuilt. The chapel is housed in the lower part of the forebuilding.

49

mined and a charge by the French captured it, the garrison withdrawing behind the main walls. Now Louis's miners got to work once more, digging another mine below the gate itself, aiming it at the eastern of the two towers flanking the passage. Several surviving short tunnels begun within the castle suggest that these are countermines dug in the vain hope of breaking into the enemy tunnel, and that either Hubert guessed that a second mine was approaching or Louis made no attempt to hide the entrance, hoping to break the morale of the defenders with this most dangerous of siege weapons.

The mine was successful, and the tower was brought down. However, all did not go as hoped for the rebels. Hubert and his men offered desperate resistance against the incursion of the rebel soldiers. His audacity paid off: perhaps the narrowness of the breach also worked in his favour, for the French were driven back and forced to quit it. Hubert then managed to block the breach with solid timber baulks and crossbeams, and the gate was never taken. The garrison made temporary repairs to the walls, while Louis found his supply trains being attacked by guerrillas from the Weald. A truce was called in the autumn, to allow fresh orders to be received from the king, but in October John died at Newark Castle, to be succeeded by his infant son, Henry III. With the truce extended, Hubert marched out. Louis passed Dover by sea the following April, to see his camp burned by the men from the Weald. He returned the following May to resume the siege, needing to protect his supply route. He now had little alternative but to use a direct assault to bring about a swift conclusion, but the French were defeated at Lincoln three days later and the war was effectively over. Louis withdrew to France, and Dover remained bloodied but unbowed. The present Norfolk Towers were built over the damaged gate, which was permanently blocked up, but evidence of the damaged original gate remains concealed behind. Hubert's spirited resistance shows that, despite a three-line defence, he did not retire to the inner bailey and certainly not the donjon, preferring to present an aggressive front even in what might appear a hopeless defensive position on the outer wall. The new concentric style of defence now beginning to make its appearance had not prevented a near disaster, unless firepower from the inner walls contributed to the discomfiture of the rebel attack. His defence also reveals that the outwork protecting the gate could not stop a determined foe. Events also swayed the siege. If the French had not been beaten in battle, would an assault on Dover have worked? We shall never know.

Bungay in Suffolk once boasted a large donjon, but following the siege of 1174 a mine was driven under one corner to destroy it. Though the threat was never carried out the entrance to the mine can still be seen.

The small donjon at Appleby in Cumbria was probably erected in the third quarter of the 12th century. The battlements appear to have been raised a little at a later date.

Roger Bigod II, the man who rebuilt Framlingham Castle, refused to support King John and, not surprisingly, he found himself under siege there in 1216 by royal foreign mercenaries. Inside the walls were 26 knights, 20 sergeants and 7 crossbowmen, plus a chaplain and three other persons. Despite its powerful towers that cut off sections of wall, its loopholes and shuttered battlements, the castle surrendered after two days. So again a major factor in the holding of a castle was the quality of the defenders. Some were tough and bloody-minded men, but the commander's word was final. On rare occasions, his word was not enough: at Bridgnorth, in 1102, the mercenaries in the garrison had to be locked up because they refused to agree to the surrender terms that the rest of the garrison were willing to accept from Henry I. Another factor was the size of a garrison. Strong walls with cunningly conceived loopholes are of little benefit if there are only seven crossbowmen to man them; and crossbows had a relatively slow rate of fire, though not as slow as later when mechanical winders became common to draw back more powerful bows. Seven men could not hope to stop an assault pressed with determination. A castle may hold off a larger force with ladders, since only one attacker can reach the wall top at a time, but a lack of archers can be fatal.

One factor that emerges from a number of sieges, both great and small, during the Norman/Angevin period, is that few castles could stand up to a prolonged siege when the king himself was determined to capture them. Even a great castle such as Rochester could not easily withstand John when the full might of royal power was brought to bear, despite members of the baronage being in revolt. Similarly a donjon was not necessarily a deterrent.

The fate of the castles

Many Norman castles continued in use following the death of John in 1216. Their curtain walls might be built over and improved, their mural towers perhaps replaced, but the essential castle often carried on as before, perhaps gradually enlarging or improving its defences. The value of the Norman castles lay not least in their positioning. So many had been well thought out by the engineers and military-minded lords that each site itself was not disturbed, though it might on occasion be enlarged. Whilst small adulterine castles (usually earth and timber structures) erected during the anarchy of Stephen's reign might be pulled down during that of his successor, Henry II, most other castles continued. Many were royal or baronial strongholds and therefore carried on as such. Their defences and domestic arrangements were to see most change and development during the following centuries. When new castles were built, notably during Edward I's invasion of Wales from the 1270s, then a new concept in design was to be seen.

The great tower or donjon became rather unfashionable during the early years of the 13th century. Rarely, existing ones might be used for defence as necessary, as witnessed by the siege of Rochester in 1215.

However, castle planning was in development. The demolished donjon at White Castle and the impressive mural towers of Framlingham foreshadowed a move away from the great tower. Defence was now becoming concentrated on the curtain walls and on powerful towers set along the walls, usually D-shaped or circular, with increasingly strong gatehouses to guard the entrance. The imposing castles of Edward I at Harlech, Caernarfon and Conway seem to have towers the size of a donjon set along the walls. Yet Edward, alongside such marvels, built Flint with a large cylindrical tower at one corner almost like a motte and bailey in layout. In Scotland John de Vaux, steward of Marie de Coucy, built Dirleton, East Lothian, in 1240: it too has a massive cylindrical tower, a veritable donjon, based on Coucy-le-Château in northern France, imitating the castle of his patron's father. A few years later Walter of Moray began work on another huge circular donjon, this time at Bothwell on the Clyde, and by the outbreak of the Wars of Independence in 1296 so much work had gone into the tower that the curtain walls were not finished.

Inside such castles accommodation was either in halls and chamber blocks, or within the wall towers, or even in rooms over the gate itself. Castles containing a donjon might find it modified to contemporary taste, as the sons of William Marshall at Chepstow did in the 13th century, who heightened the old donjon and replaced the windows. Here too, towards the end of the century a new domestic range was added in the bailey. The ideas of the hall with attached service rooms and of a kitchen with its passage flanked by pantry and buttery were coming in.

Similarly the modest donjon at Goodrich is tucked within the huge walls and cylindrical towers of the

The curtain wall at Brough, Cumbria, is of the 11th century, but the present donjon was built to replace the one destroyed in the siege of 1174.

The curtain walls of White Castle, Gwent, were probably built between 1184 and 1186. The old donjon, visible as a square of stone in the grass, was demolished in the 13th century when new circular towers were added.

13th-century castle, as defence was based increasingly on front-line tactics and more up-to-date domestic ranges were required.

The donjon might still cause a problem to the authorities as late as the 17th century, when some castles were besieged. Even after a victorious siege, the attackers sometimes encountered difficulty when destroying these huge towers; but wreck them they did, as witness the great tower at Corfe Castle, or that still hanging precariously at an angle at Bridgnorth, Shropshire.

There were, moreover, far too many donjons in existence simply to ignore them, and they carried on being used for various purposes. The White Tower was still in use for royal meetings in the late-15th century, and if a famous illustration is to be believed, was deemed comfortable enough to house the Duke of Orleans for a time, following his capture at Agincourt in 1415. When the kings no longer stayed in the Tower, except before their coronation, the White Tower became a convenient giant storehouse, and the majority of the original small windows were enlarged in about 1700 to increase the available light and air. New doors were also knocked through. Many donjons similarly fell into disuse except as convenient storehouses for materials. However, the strategic importance of some castles meant that they were adapted for more modern usage. At the White Tower vaults were inserted into the basement, to allow heavy guns to be mounted on the roof, and this was to be the fate of several castles' donjons. Dover, on its cliff over the Channel, also had vaults inserted in the 1790s and the roof flattened, while Carlisle had the battlements reshaped in-line with those seen in gun emplacements.

The idea of the donjon or tower never really disappeared. Large residential tower-houses continued to be built as private residences for the lord and his immediate family, such as that at the late-14th-century Percy stronghold of Warkworth in Northumberland. The walls were now pierced with more windows and provided with more domestic rooms internally. One of the best known is that of the Cromwell family erected in 1450 at Tattershall in Lincolnshire. In areas of unrest, such as border areas of Scotland, or in Ireland, these residential towers still had a certain military air, with rooms stacked on top of one another. They could protect a family against cattle thieves and small-scale attacks, but were not really designed to withstand a siege. As such they remained in use until the 17th century, long after castles themselves had given way to fortresses manned by guns and garrisons only.

Visiting the castles today

It would be impossible to give full details of all the many Norman castles that can be visited in the limited space available, so a selective treatment follows, focusing on those mentioned in the text. 'CADW' is the acronym of the Welsh Historic Monuments organisation.

Appleby-in-Westmorland, Cumbria (private, but open to the public). From the A66, continue into the town on the B6260: the castle stands on a hill above the town centre, within a loop of the River Eden. It has a well-preserved donjon. Nearby is a rare-breed centre.

Arundel, West Sussex (the seat of the Duke of Norfolk, open to the public). Off the A27 between Chichester and Worthing, the castle has been much restored, having been in constant occupation since the 11th century. The village is also worth visiting.

Bamburgh, Northumberland (private, but open to the public). The castle is situated on a cliff and can be accessed from the village on the B1341, turning off the A1. The most majestic view, made famous by films and calendars, is from the beach below, however. The donjon has been much altered and furnished inside, making it difficult to trace the original parts. The Grace Darling Museum can also be visited in the village.

Barnard Castle, Co. Durham (English Heritage). On the A67, the castle has a cylindrical tower dating to about 1200, with other medieval buildings. The Bowes Museum is nearby.

Berkeley, Gloucestershire (private, but open to the public). Berkeley is on the B4509, reached via the A38 or M5. The castle consists of a motte with two baileys, the motte concealed within Norman walls. There is a 14th-century domestic range in the eastern bailey.

The interior of Framlingham, Suffolk, built about 1180, showing the open-backed towers and the archers' embrasures in the walls.

N

0 50 miles
0 100 km

SCOTLAND

NORTH
SEA

Castle Sween

Norham

Bamburgh

Carlisle
Newcastle upon Tyne
Prudhoe

Brougham
Appleby
Brough Barnard Castle
Carrickfergus Bowes Richmond
Middleham
Scarborough
Helmsley

IRELAND

IRISH SEA

Trim

Conisbrough

Nenagh

Newark

ENGLAND

Oakham
Castle Acre
Castle Rising
Norwich
New Buckenham
Bungay

Clun
Ludlow
Kenilworth
Framlingham
Orford
Colchester

WALES

Castle Hedingham

Grosmont
Skenfrith
Tretower Goodrich
White Castle
Chepstow Berkeley
Oxford
Tower of
London
Rochester
Pembroke
Bridgend

Windsor
Guildford Eynsford Canterbury
Farnham West Dover
Malling

Winchester
Portchester
Pevensey

Sherborne
Arundel

Okehampton
Christchurch
Launceston Exeter Carisbrooke
Restormel Corfe Castle
Totnes

ENGLISH CHANNEL

The location of the key Norman
stone castles in the British Isles
featured in this work.

FRANCE

55

The donjon and walls of Carrickfergus, Antrim, were built in the late-12th century. (Crown Copyright; reproduced with permission of the Controller, HMSO)

Carlisle, Cumbria (English Heritage). Approached from the A595, this castle lies on the northern outskirts of the medieval walled town. It was occupied until the 19th century and therefore contains buildings of several periods. The castle consists of an inner and outer bailey, and the Norman remains include the donjon and parts of the curtain walls. The original door into the donjon has been blocked and a ground floor entrance is now used. One side of the donjon has been thinned and covered by a new wall.

Carrickfergus, Co. Antrim (Environment & Heritage Service: Built Heritage). Eight miles north-east of Belfast on the A2. One of the largest Irish castles, Carrickfergus is a long, narrow castle on the peninsula in Belfast Lough. It was host to King John during his visit to the country in 1210.

Castle Acre, Norfolk (English Heritage). Castle Acre (the town and castle share the same name) is reached via the A1065: the castle and town gate lay at the north end of the town. From the castle, an easy walk through the town brings you to the Norman priory ruins, with a superb west front.

Castle Hedingham, Essex (private, but open to the public). The village is reached via the B1058; the castle lies just to the north of it. The tower is well worth a visit, though only earthworks survive otherwise.

Castle Rising, Norfolk (English Heritage). Best reached by car, 5.5 miles north-west of King's Lynn on the A149.

Colchester, Essex (borough council). Situated on the A12, the castle stands just north of the high street in the town. It now houses the Colchester and Essex Museum.

Conisbrough, Yorkshire (English Heritage). On the A630 between Sheffield and Doncaster, the castle stands in the centre of the town, and is largely a 12th-century ruin.

Corfe Castle, Dorset (English Heritage). Situated on the A351, but the preserved Dorset Light Railway also has a station in the village. Best reached by parking in the car parks on the village outskirts and walking to the castle ruins through the village, which is charming. The castle perches on a ridge above the village.

Dover, Kent (English Heritage). Dover is situated on a height on the eastern outskirts of the town, off the A2. If using a car, be prepared for traffic queues approaching the town and port, especially during holiday periods.

Dover Priory railway station is located in the town, from where a taxi can be hired, or the more energetic can hike to the castle. Parking is within the earthworks, and most of the castle can be explored, though there are numerous later additions to the fabric, especially dating from the Napoleonic and Victorian periods. There is a restaurant within the inner bailey that gives a good view of the wall fabric. Most of the battlements have either been renewed or lost when towers were cut in size. The donjon windows are mainly of Edward IV's time, as are other internal insertions, while barrel vaults on the top floor and other insertions date from the 1700s.

Framlingham, Suffolk (English Heritage). Located north of Ipswich on the B1120, the castle is in the centre of the village in Christchurch Park. The castle shop offers free hire of a useful audio tour pack for the wall walk.

Grosmont, Gwent (CADW). This castle forms part of the 'Three Castles' given to Hubert de Burgh in 1201, together with Skenfrith and White Castle. It lies on the B4347 some two miles from Pontrilas. There is a first-floor stone hall of about 1150 within a towered enclosure.

Helmsley, North Yorkshire (English Heritage). The castle is in the town centre, some 20 miles north of York on the A170. It is set on a curtain wall, and a Tudor range stands in the enclosure.

Kenilworth, Warwickshire. Reached from the A46 south-west of Coventry. The impressive donjon in red sandstone was poorly altered by Robert Dudley, Earl of Leicester, and slighted in the 17th century. Dudley also built a complex of buildings, and the castle was the scene of a lavish visit by Elizabeth I. The 14th-century hall of John of Gaunt also survives.

The donjon of Carrickfergus, Antrim. (Crown Copyright; reproduced with permission of the Controller, HMSO)

Launceston, Cornwall (English Heritage). Launceston lies off the A30, west of Exeter. It is largely intact, apart from later interference with the motte on which the shell keep and 13th-century tower sit.

Ludlow, Shropshire (borough council). Reached via the A49 or A4117, the town of Ludlow contains a number of interesting old buildings. As well as the Norman donjon on the old gate and the circular chapel, the castle has a 14th-century hall complex and Mortimer's Tower, as well as displaying 16th- and 17th-century work.

Middleham, North Yorkshire (English Heritage). Reached via the A6108 from Leyburn: the large donjon is set closely within a fortified enclosure of the 13th and 14th centuries. One of its famous owners was the Earl of Warwick, 'the Kingmaker'. The original motte and bailey can be seen to the south-west.

Newcastle upon Tyne, Tyne and Wear (City of Newcastle). In the centre of the city, off the A69: the castle can also be seen from the train that passes remarkably close to its walls. An impressive donjon with basement chapel; there is a bagpipe museum in the gatehouse.

Norham, Northumberland (English Heritage). On the A698 and B6470 from Berwick-upon-Tweed. There are defences of all

Launceston in Cornwall has a motte (slightly distorted through later modification) on which lies a 12th-century shell keep with wing walls. The circular tower inside was added in the 13th century.

periods from the 12th to 16th centuries. The donjon was altered in the 15th century.

Norwich, Norfolk (City of Norwich). The castle on its hill stands in the middle of the city: if arriving by car it is best to use the park-and-ride facilities. Much of the donjon was refaced in the 19th century, though following the original layout. It now houses displays from Norwich Museum.

Orford, Suffolk (English Heritage). Best reached by car, it lies eight miles east of Woodbridge on the B1084. Go through the village to the site car park. The remains are of the donjon set within its earthworks.

Pembroke, Dyfed (CADW). Reached via the A4139 or the A4075, the castle is perched above the river to the north-west of the city centre. The donjon sits within a large enclosure surrounded by 13th-century defences.

Portchester, Hampshire (English Heritage). Portchester is situated on the south coast, four miles east of Fareham, off the A27. It stands in the corner of a Roman fort, with a 12th-century Augustinian priory in the opposite corner. The donjon was given an additional two storeys some time before 1250.

Restormel, Cornwall (English Heritage). Reached from the B3268 south of Bodmin or the A390 from Lostwithiel: Restormel Castle is set on a low mound on the west bank of the Fowey. The 12th-century shell keep contains the remains of 13th-century domestic buildings inside.

Richmond, Yorkshire (English Heritage). On the A6136, west of the A1, the castle stands in the centre of Richmond, just off the market place: it gives good views over the River Swale below.

Rochester, Kent (English Heritage). Rochester Castle lies on the river in the centre of Rochester by Bridge Reach: the city can be accessed by train, or by car via the A2. The castle site is large, but much of the Norman curtain and mural towers have been overbuilt or destroyed. A visit to the donjon is well worth it, though the window openings have suffered. There is no replacement flooring internally, and those with no head for heights may find the views from the window embrasures a little unsettling. The rebuilt rounded corner is perhaps best viewed by walking round the road outside the castle. The Norman cathedral is only a short walk from the castle too.

Scarborough, Yorkshire (English Heritage). The A170 or the coastal A165 lead to Scarborough. The ruins are perched on a headland on the east side of the town but can be reached on foot if necessary.

Sherborne Old Castle, Dorset (English Heritage). Reached via the A30 or the A352, the Norman castle is not to be confused with the new (Tudor) castle next door. The old castle lies on the eastern outskirts of the town, and there is ample parking. Sherborne Abbey is also worth visiting in the town itself.

Skenfrith, Gwent (CADW). Situated on the B4521, the castle is relatively unspoiled.

Tower of London (Historic Royal Palaces). There are no visitor parking facilities except for a nearby multi-storey paying car park, so it is best to arrive by the Underground (Tower Hill on the Circle and District Line being the closest stop) or else by bus or taxi. Small sections of the Roman city wall are still visible, but the Conqueror's ditch is filled in. The White Tower now houses displays by the Royal Armouries. On the north side additional entrances have latterly been inserted. All the windows were enlarged in about 1700 except for a small pair above the entrance, and a blocked pair beside them that lit the passage. The top floor was inserted in the 1490s, so the floor below does not look as it did during Norman times. Outside is the stump of the 12th-century Wardrobe Tower, on the line of the Roman city wall (represented by 'tram lines' in the grass). The late-12th-century polygonal Bell Tower is normally closed but can be viewed from the outside. The Crown Jewels are, of course, also displayed in the Tower. There is a restaurant in the New Armouries building, and plenty of seating, though the castle can become very busy during the summer months.

Trim, Co. Meath. Situated 23 miles north-west of Dublin on the L3 off the N3. The donjon is sited in a triangular bailey with curtain wall and towers.

White Castle, Gwent (CADW). The castle is on the B4233, six miles east of Abergavenny. The 12th-century walls, which remain in good condition, have 13th-century towers and a gatehouse.

Windsor, Surrey (Historic Royal Palaces). Reached by train or via the B3022, the castle lies in the centre of town. It consists of two very large baileys with a motte between. The shell keep was rebuilt by Edward III, and was raised and restored by George IV in the 19th century. Much of the original castle is built over but offers plenty of interest, notably the royal tombs in the 15th-century St George's Chapel, home of the Knights of the Garter.

Restormel in Cornwall is a shell keep probably of the late-12th century, set on a shallow motte, with 13th-century buildings abutting the walls inside.

Bibliography

Among the most important sources of information on individual castles are the guidebooks produced for each site. These can be obtained during visits, but are too numerous to list below. Those published by English Heritage and CADW can also be ordered through their retail outlets.

Allen Brown, R. *English Castles* (2nd edition, London, 1976)
>   (ed.) *Castles: A History and Guide* (London, 1980)
>   *The Architecture of Castles* (London, 1984)
>   *Castles from the Air* (Cambridge, 1989)
Anderson, W.F.D. *Castles of Europe* (London, 1970)
Armitage, E. *Early Norman Castles of the British Isles* (London, 1912)
Bradbury, Jim *The Medieval Siege* (Woodbridge, 1992)
Coad, J.G. and Streeten, A.D.F. 'Excavations at Castle Acre Castle, Norfolk 1972–77: Country House and Castle of the Norman Earls of Surrey', *Archaeological Journal*, CXXXIX, pp138–302 (1982)
Coad, Jonathan *Book of Dover Castle* (London, 1995)
Clapham, AW *Romanesque Architecture in Western Europe* (Oxford, 1936)
Colvin, H.M., Brown, R.A. and Taylor, A.J. *The History of the King's Works, The Middle Ages*, 2 vols (London, 1963)
Coulson, C. 'Peaceable Power in Norman Castles', *Anglo-Norman Studies*, Vol. XXIII, pp69–95 (2001)
Counihan, J.M. 'Mrs Ella Armitage, John Horace Round, G.T. Clark and Early Norman Castles', *Anglo-Norman Studies*, Vol. VIII, pp73–87 (1986)
Cruden, S. *The Scottish Castle*, 3rd edition (Edinburgh, 1981)

An interior view of the circular tower at Barnard Castle, County Durham, *c.*1200, built of sandstone ashlar. The basement has a spirally built rubble dome. The castle withstood a siege by Alexander of Scotland in 1216.

Davison, B.K. 'The Origins of the Castle in England', *Archaeological Journal*, Vol. CXXIV, pp202–11 (1967)

Dixon, Philip 'The Myth of the Keep', *The Seigneurial Residence in Western Europe AD c800-1600*, BAR International Series 1088, pp9–13 (Oxford, 2002)

Gies, Joseph and Gies, Frances *Life in a Medieval Castle* (London, 1975)

Goodall, J. 'Dover Castle and the Siege of 1216', *Château Gaillard*, Vol. XIX, pp91–202 (2000)

Gravett, Christopher *The History of Castles* (Guilford, CT, 2001)

'Kitchens and Keeps: Domestic Arrangements in Norman Castles', *Royal Armouries Yearbook*, Vol. III, pp168–75 (Leeds, 1998)

'Siege Warfare in Orderic Vitalis', *Royal Armouries Yearbook*, Vol. V, pp139–47 (Leeds, 2000)

Guy, John *Kent Castles* (Gillingham, 1980)

Holland, P. 'The Anglo-Normans and their Castles in County Galway', *Galway: History and Society*, ed. G. Moran and R. Gillespie, p126 (Dublin, 1996)

'The Anglo-Norman Landscape in County Galway: Landholding, Castles and Settlements', *Journal of the Galway Archaeological and Historical Society*, Vol. XLIX, pp159–93 (1997)

Impey, Edward and Harris, Roland 'Boothby Pagnall Revisited', *The Seigneurial Residence in Western Europe AD c800-1600*, BAR International Series 1088, pp245–269 (Oxford, 2002)

Kenyon, John R. *Medieval Fortifications* (Leicester, 1990)

Leask, H.G. *Irish Castles and Castellated Houses*, 3rd edition (Dundalk, 1977)

Lindsay, M. *The Castles of Scotland* (London, 1986)

Marshall, Pamela 'The Great Tower as Residence', *The Seigneurial Residence in Western Europe AD c800-1600*, BAR International Series 1088, pp27–44 (Oxford, 2002)

McNeill, Tom *Castles* (London, 1992)

Moore, J. 'Anglo-Norman Garrisons', *Anglo-Norman Studies*, Vol. XXII, (2000)

Morillo, S. *Warfare under the Anglo-Norman Kings, 1066-1135* (Woodbridge, 1994)

Parnell, Geoffrey *The Tower of London* (London, 1993)

Pettifer, Adrian *English Castles: a Guide by Counties* (Woodbridge, 1995)

Welsh Castles: a Guide by Counties (Woodbridge, 2000)

Phillips, G. *Scottish Castles* (Glasgow, 1987)

Platt, Colin *The Castle in Medieval England and Wales* (London, 1982)

Renn, Derek *Norman Castles in Britain* (London, 1968)

Rowley, Trevor *The Norman Heritage, 1066-1200* (London, 1983)

Saunders, A.D. (co-ord.), *Five Castle Excavations* (RAI, London, 1978)

Tabraham, Christopher *Scottish Castles and Fortifications* (HMSO, Edinburgh, 1986)

Thompson, M.W. *The Rise of the Castle* (Cambridge, 1991)

'Keep or Country House? Thin-Walled Norman "Proto-Keeps"', *Fortress*, Vol. 12, pp13–22 (February 1992)

'The Military Interpretation of Castles', *Archaeological Journal*, Vol. CLI, pp439–45 (1994)

Toy, Sidney *Castles: Their Construction and History* (London, 1939)

Tuulse, A. *Castles of the Western World* (London, 1958)

White, P. 'Castle Gateways During the Reign of Henry II', *Antiquaries Journal*, Vol. LXXVI, pp241–7 (1996)

Wood, M.E. *The English Medieval House* (London, 1965)

The great round tower at Pembroke was built in about 1200.

Glossary

Apse A rounded end.

Ashlar Smooth, flat masonry blocks.

Bailey A courtyard.

Ballista A projectile engine resembling a giant crossbow, utilising the tension of a bow or the torsion of two arms thrust through skeins of cord. Usually used for shooting large arrows or bolts.

Bar hole A hole in a wall into which a drawbar slides.

Barbican An outwork that protects a gate.

Barrel vault A cylindrical plain stone vault.

Batter The base of a wall thickened with a sloping front.

Belfry A wooden tower, often mobile, used either to overlook a wall or to transfer troops on to it.

Berm The space between a wall and ditch.

Brattice Wooden hoarding built out from a battlement to command the base of a wall.

Buttress Stone support built against a wall to reinforce it.

Chemise A wall closely surrounding a donjon.

Corbel A supporting stone bracket.

Countermine A tunnel dug from a castle aimed at breaking into an enemy mineshaft.

Counterscarp The outer slope of a ditch.

Crenel The open section of a battlement.

Crenellation Battlement.

The circular tower at Skenfrith, Gwent, dates to the early-13th century.

Cross-vault A vault in which two barrel vaults intersect.

Curtain A length of wall surrounding a castle enclosure.

Donjon A great tower or keep, but it can also mean an upper bailey or lord's private area.

Drawbar A wooden beam for securing the inside of a door, which runs back into a hole in the wall to allow the door to open.

Embrasure An internal opening in a wall, sometimes for the use of archers.

Enceinte The area enclosed by the castle walls.

Forebuilding A stone building erected against the side of a donjon to cover the entrance.

Great tower A keep.

Groined vault A cross-vault whose edges are sharply defined.

Hoarding see **Brattice**.

Jamb The side of an opening through a wall.

Joggled Keyed together by overlapping joints.

Keep The word used in England from the 16th century to describe a donjon or great tower.

Loop A narrow opening in a wall that splays out internally, designed either to admit light or for shooting through.

Machicolation Battlement brought forward on corbels to allow soldiers to command the base of a wall.

Mangonel Variously used to describe a torsion catapult utilising a skein of cord as a spring, or a trebuchet, often the type utilising manpower.

Merlon The solid section of a battlement.

Mine A tunnel dug under a wall to weaken the foundations and bring it down.

Moat A ditch, either wet or dry.

Motte An earth mound.

Mural chamber A vaulted chamber formed in the thickness of a wall.

Mural passage A vaulted passage formed in the thickness of a wall.

Mural tower A tower set along a curtain wall.

Parados A low, inner wall of a wall-walk.

Parapet The outer wall of a wall-walk.

Petrary A stone-throwing catapult.

Pilaster A shallow pier built against a wall to buttress it.

Portcullis A lattice made from wood clad in iron, or occasionally in iron alone, dropped to block a gate.

Postern A small rear door.

Rampart An earthen bank.

Revetment The side of a ditch, bank or motte faced with wood, stone or brick.

Ring-work A circular or oval earthwork with bank and ditch.

Scarp The side of a ditch.

Shell keep A motte in which the timber palisade on the summit is replaced by a stone wall.

Spur A solid, pointed stone reinforcement at the base of a tower; also, a finger of high ground.

Turning bridge A bridge like a see-saw, the rear half falling into a pit as the front section is raised.

Trebuchet A catapult whose throwing arm utilises the principle of counterbalance.

Turret A small tower.

Vault A curved ceiling of stone.

Vice A spiral stair.

Wall-walk A passage along the top of a wall.

Ward see **Bailey**.

Wing-wall A wall descending the slope of a motte.

Tretower is a small circular tower erected between 1174 and 1220.

Index

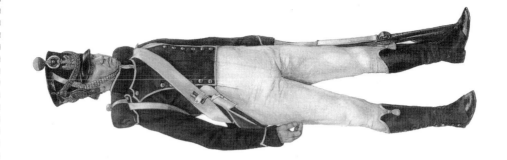

OSPREY
PUBLISHING

FIND OUT MORE ABOUT OSPREY

❑ Please send me the latest listing of Osprey's publications

❑ I would like to subscribe to Osprey's e-mail newsletter

Title / rank

Name

Address

City / county

Postcode / zip   state / country

e-mail

I am interested in:

❑ Ancient world
❑ Medieval world
❑ 16th century
❑ 17th century
❑ 18th century
❑ Napoleonic
❑ 19th century

❑ American Civil War
❑ World War 1
❑ World War 2
❑ Modern warfare
❑ Military aviation
❑ Naval warfare

Please send to:

USA & Canada:
Osprey Direct USA, c/o MBI Publishing, P.O. Box 1,
729 Prospect Avenue, Osceola, WI 54020

UK, Europe and rest of world:
Osprey Direct UK, P.O. Box 140, Wellingborough,
Northants, NN8 2FA, United Kingdom

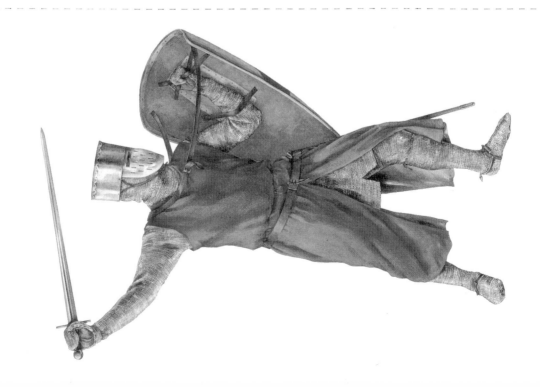

OSPREY
PUBLISHING

www.ospreypublishing.com

call our telephone hotline
for a free information pack

USA & Canada: 1-800-826-6600
UK, Europe and rest of world call:
+44 (0) 1933 443 863

Young Guardsman
Figure taken from Warrior 22:
Imperial Guardsman 1799–1815
Published by Osprey
Illustrated by Christa Hook

Knight, c.1190
Figure taken from *Warrior 1: Norman Knight 950 – 1204 AD*
Published by Osprey
Illustrated by Christa Hook

POSTCARD